Creation Science

Confirming that the Bible is right

David Rosevear

New Wine Press

© 1991 David Rosevear

New Wine Press
PO Box 17
Chichester
England PO20 6YB

We thank Mr Brian Newton of Matlock for illustrations on pages 27 and 89.
Illustrations on pages 51, 107, 109, 118, 119, 121 and 122 are from *Fossil Man*, by Frank W. Cousins, published by the Creation Science Movement.

ISBN 0 947852 91 3

Typeset by CRB Typesetting Services, Ely, Cambs.
Printed by Richard Clay Ltd, Bungay, Suffolk

Contents

Contents

Page

Dedication

To Joan,

*whose walk with the
Lord and obsessive
love of His word
have been a source
of inspiration to me
during forty years.*

D.R.

Illustrations

8

Introduction

The doctrine of Special Creation, as opposed to evolution theory, is foundational to the doctrines of original sin, redemption through the death of Christ, and the final restoration of all things. At first sight it may seem that the creation versus evolution argument is a side issue. It is a matter for the scientific specialists. It has no apparent bearing on our eternal salvation, and it is possible to believe in evolution theory and still be a good Christian.

Surveys among students and the general population have shown that the major reason why people reject Christianity is that they think that science has proved the Bible to be unreliable, especially with regard to origins.

We shall show that evolution theory is the scientific arm of atheistic humanism. Its general acceptance has been accompanied by a decline in church attendance, a revision of the absolute standards contained in the moral code, and a change in attitudes towards the value of human life both before birth and late in life. Recognizing the relationship between evolutionary philosophy and moral decline, some have sought to harmonize the theory of evolution with the biblical revelation. Compromise positions will be discussed.

Naturally, if the theory of evolution could be shown to be true, based on scientific observation and in line with scientific laws, we should need to review our belief in the inerrancy of God's Word, or our interpretation of it. However, what is not generally appreciated is that evolution theory cannot interpret the observations, that it is contrary to basic laws of science, and is recognized by many scientists as being untenable.

We shall discuss the scientific evidence for Creation and against evolution. The proposed spontaneous formation of a first living cell and the subsequent evolution of such a cell into other life forms, are contrary to the principles of genetics and molecular biology . All living things confirm the work of a Designer. We shall consider some design features to show that they rule out a chance origin or development. The fossils support a recent creation and world-wide Flood. That the earth and the universe are only thousands of years old will be considered. The fanciful evidence for ape-men will be exposed.

The evidence of Scripture will be discussed. The Bible contains many scientific facts only recently confirmed by man's discoveries. Further, the New Testament writers show the importance of a literal Adam and Eve. Most importantly, the Creator Himself, the Lord Jesus Christ speaks of Adam and Eve being made 'in the beginning' and couples their son, Abel, with reference to the foundation of the world.

We shall show that Jeremiah's conclusion that God made the earth by His power, He founded the world by His wisdom and stretched out the heavens by His understanding, is more satisfactory than the contention that in the beginning was a big bang, that life formed spontaneously in some primaeval pond, and proliferated by chance mutations selected by a changing environment.

Chapter 1

Creation or Evolution – Does it really matter?

At school, on radio and TV, and in text-books, encyclo-paedias and children's books on the wonders of nature, we are bombarded with evolution theory. It is put across as though it were all proven fact; in effect to doubt it is to be anti-intellectual. Cavemen are depicted as ape-like. Dino-saurs are said to have become extinct 65 million years ago. Life arose spontaneously at least a thousand million years BP (Before Present) and the universe began with a Big Bang perhaps fifteen billion years ago. A blind purposeless process has produced, over vast aeons of time, all the diversity of plant and animal life, culminating in purposeful man. With man slowly improving from the brute beast, by way of the noble savage, to Mr Homo Sapiens Sapiens, the future for the race is bright indeed. 'Oh brave new world that hath such creatures in it!'

Truth of Scripture

The Christian, having been brain-washed from birth by this world-view, can find it difficult to believe that God made everything, plants, fish, birds, beasts and man, all in less than a week.

The natural reaction is to say that science must be right, and that the Genesis account is primitive folk-lore. Maybe

11

A book of the Torah.

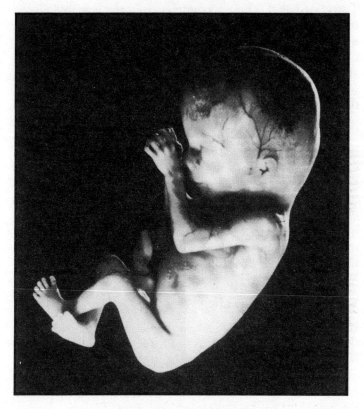

Eight week old embryo (twice life size).

Genesis uses myth to say that God is behind everything, and this serves to introduce a code of morality and law which is a useful guide, even today.

By this reasoning, we also reject as naive the story of a world-wide Flood and the confusion of languages at the Tower of Babel. These accounts convey the laudable notion of a holy God, but are considered by many scholars to be not very different from legends. And then, having begun to question the truth of scripture, we must ask what we think about the stories of miracles in the Gospels. In particular, what about the Resurrection, the Ascension, Pentecost and the promised Second Coming? When we start to dismiss the opening chapters of the Bible, where do we stop?

The Psalmist says that *'Thy Word is true from the beginning'*. Paul claims that *'all Scripture is inspired by God'*. Jesus Christ Himself points out that the Scripture cannot be broken, and guarantees that neither a jot nor a tittle will in any wise pass from the law until all is fulfilled. A jot was the smallest letter of the Hebrew alphabet. The tittle was a small horn-like appendage which transformed one Hebrew letter into another. The very letters of the original Scriptures were God's changeless Word.

Sanctity of Human Life

If evolution theory is true, and the Garden of Eden a myth, then it follows that man was not made in the image of God. What is so special about human life? An unwanted foetus can be aborted. Evolutionists used to say that a human embryo recapitulates its evolutionary ancestry, passing through a fish-like stage with gill slits. Today scientists know this is not so, but the idea persists. We kill fish, so why not abort a human foetus? But no need to stop there. We can 'mercy kill' a badly deformed child at birth: and when folk have out-lived their usefulness they can be eliminated with dignity, thus avoiding unnecessary suffering (and, incidentally, expense).

The fertilized egg has all the potential, with no further input of genetic information, to develop into a person made in the image of God. The Psalmist points out that God knit him together in his mother's womb; that God's eyes saw his substance, being yet unformed. Job, Isaiah, Jeremiah and Paul all say that God called them from the womb, as does the Messianic Psalm 22. Today the 'slaughter of the innocents' in abortion clinics is an affront to the One who said *'Thou shalt not kill'*. But to the evolutionist it is of less concern than the culling of seals.

Racism

If man came down from the trees, some races are closer to the apes than others. Such peoples are less advanced. Sir Arthur Keith has pointed out that Hitler's racist views sprang naturally from Darwinism. Both Darwin and Huxley, in their published letters, expressed racist views, for example against Turks and negroes. Following the exposure of the horrific consequences of Nazi racism, the climate of opinion was sympathetic to a civil rights movement and the passing of laws against incitement to racial hatred. The scientific aspect was no longer voiced. However, by the close of the nineteen eighties, men such as Professor Rushton in the States were again attempting to relate brain size to intelligence. He claims that orientals are more advanced than caucasians, who in turn are a more highly evolved race than negroes. (It is of interest that many fossil men such as Cro-Magnon and Neanderthal men had greater brain capacities than today's average.) One has to ask whether I.Q. tests can fairly reflect mental ability, let alone wisdom. In making comparisons between ethnic groups, one has also to take account of social and economic factors. Mental agility is strongly influenced by general health, which in turn depends on diet and medical care.

Only allegiance to the evolutionary world-view enables one to conclude that some races are inherently more

Variations within a species.

advanced or primitive. There is no evidence for this, and all the evidence confirms that mankind is a single species. Given the same opportunities, men of different races have, on average, the same potential, mentally, physically and spiritually. Genesis 11 gives the origin of the nations, and Paul, speaking to the intellectual elite of his day, as reported in Acts 17, reaffirms that God has made of one all nations of men. Today, geneticists are coming to the same conclusion from a study of human mitochondrial DNA.

Can an Evolutionist Sin?

If the Fall is a legend, what is sin? The transgression of whose law? The 'Ten Commandments' was a set of rules imposed by the establishment class upon the lower orders in order to preserve the status quo. Whatever is good for the survival of the fittest must be right. Sin becomes what is socially unacceptable; sin against the environment. Thus deviant acts between consenting adults cannot be wrong, if we are the product of blind chance out of natural selection.

If man is a product of chance, then behaviour is a matter of expediency. What strange quirk of evolution made man with a sense of right and wrong, but a natural inclination to choose the 'wrong'? A 'survival of the fittest' philosophy knows only the law of the jungle. Decent chaps come last. Those evolutionists who help the weak and behave in an altruistic way are not really being very consistent with this philosophy!

Salvation from What?

If man has not fallen, he has no need of a Redeemer. Redemption, the central theme of the Old and New Testaments, is no more than primitive superstition, priestly mumbo-jumbo. If evolution is true, we must throw away more than Genesis. Paul says that as in Adam all die, even so in Christ shall all be made alive. Adam and Christ are contrasted in 1 Corinthians 15. The Fall is the reason for the redemption brought about only through the death and resurrection of Christ.

Death before Adam?

Adam's sin brought death, according to several passages of Scripture. Romans 5 tells us that *'through one man sin entered the world, and death through sin, and thus death spread to all men, because all sinned'*, and that *'by the one man's offence death reigned'*. Again, 1 Corinthians 15 says; *'For since by man came death, by Man also came the resurrection of the dead. For as in Adam all die, even so in Christ all shall be made alive'*. Romans 8 tells us that the creation was subjected to futility, the bondage of corruption (or death and decay). Death and corruption of not only man, but of the whole of creation, sprang from Adam's disobedience. This is set out clearly in Genesis 3.

In Adam all die. So death was not present before Adam sinned, if the Scriptures mean anything at all. This rules out evolution with its death and struggle. This also rules out the day-age compromise and the gap theory compromise. Both of these interpretations require many deaths over assumed vast periods of time before the creation of Adam.

When God had made Adam, He 'saw everything that He had made, and indeed it was very good.' If there had been struggle, death and decay before Adam, how could a just Creator see that all was very good? Theistic evolution and other compromises that allow for death before Adam are a libel against the character of the Almighty.

Meaning and Purpose

The evolutionary world-view of blind chance producing the watch, as with Dawkin's *The Blind Watchmaker*, is very unsatisfactory because it leaves no room for meaning and purpose in life. According to this philosophy, death is the end of existence for the individual, though it is the means of progress for the species. For the Christian, death leads to glory. When we see Him we shall be like Him! Death enabled God to die for the sin of man. By His resurrection, death is swallowed up in victory!

Theistic Evolution?

But can we have our cake and eat it? Can we believe in a God who used evolution to bring about his plan? What kind of god would this be?

– He would be a god who does not say what he means or mean what he says. The order of creation in Genesis is all wrong and the time scale is preposterous. He said he made plants according to their kind, with their seed within themselves to reproduce according to their kind. He said he made animals according to their kind also. If God used evolution, this account in Genesis is plain wrong.

– He is a god who uses death, struggle and chance to achieve his purposes – a cruel, gambling god.

– He takes billions of years to make man in his own image – an inefficient god.

Compromises of creation and evolution must find billions of years for the slow development of life. Genesis 1 says that all was complete in the span of one week. This presents no problem to one who believes in a powerful and wise God. Genesis 1 is historical prose, just like the rest of Genesis. The only verse which has poetic form is verse 27;

> 'So God created man in his own image,
> in the image of God created he him;
> male and female created he them.'

All the remainder of the account is sober prose, intended, of course, to be read as history. Further, Exodus 20, the Ten Commandments, states boldly that in six days the Lord made heaven and earth, the sea and all that in them is. The point is emphasized by repetition in Exodus 31, where it is pointed out that this was written with the finger of God. Hebrews 4, verse 3, referring to the sabbath rest, says that God's works were finished from the foundation of the world. This verse can not be squared with theistic evolution. We have already mentioned Matthew 19 (He that made them in the beginning), and Luke 11 (Abel and the foundation of the world). There are some dozen such verses of Scripture which refer to men going back to the beginning. Theistic evolution, Gap theory nor Day-age theory can accommodate a straightforward reading of these verses.

In the course of the next few chapters one other good reason will be offered as to why we should reject any form of theistic evolution. Evolution is unscientific.

Chapter 2

Creation and Scientific Laws

The study of science is only possible because the structures and interactions of matter are governed by immutable laws. We are able to predict the timing of the tides because the moon is subject to unchanging laws of motion and gravity. We can set up an industrial plant to manufacture, say iron, secure in the knowledge that the conditions of reduction from its ore will not arbitrarily change. Laws of science are tested. No one has observed a situation where they do not apply. For example, the weightlessness of the astronaut is not due to a break-down of the law of gravity, but to the weakness of the Earth's gravitational field in that circumstance.

Science deals in theories as well as laws. Where a theory is unable to explain all the observations, it may be modified or even scrapped. Creation and evolution are usually regarded as theories. Both are explanations of origins of the Universe, life and living forms; origins which no human has observed.

We can consider the proposed mechanisms of each of these theories to see if the laws of science are obeyed or flouted by the proposals.

Laws of Thermodynamics

The laws governing the relationship between heat and work (thermodynamics in the jargon of science), were formulated during the nineteenth century around the same time that evolution theory was replacing creation as a scientific explanation of origins. The scientist Joule, (who has given his name to the unit of energy), accurately measured the conversion of mechanical energy into heat. In the eighteenth century, Lavoisier had weighed the products of combustion to show that there was no overall weight loss when things burned. Observations of these kinds enabled the First Law of Thermodynamics to be formulated. It states that matter and energy cannot be created or destroyed. Energy can be converted from one kind to another, as from electrical energy to light and heat, but the change does not result in any gain or loss of energy. Similarly, matter can change form as when wood and oxygen burn to ash and gases, but there is no overall gain or loss of matter. In the twentieth century it was found that matter could be converted into energy by nuclear reaction, and Blackett used energy to create matter. But there is a fixed equivalence between them ($E=Mc^2$) and the sum total of matter and energy cannot be changed.

Let us apply the first law of thermodynamics to the question of the origin of the universe. Since matter and energy cannot be created or destroyed, it follows that there is nothing in the universe capable of bringing the universe into being. Of course, the universe may always have existed, but if it had a beginning it must have been created by Something outside of the universe. This latter alternative is the creationist postulate.

The Second Law of Thermodynamics, formulated as a result of studies by scientists such as Carnot and Clausius in the nineteenth century, states that in an isolated system, spontaneous processes lead to a decrease in order. Things move in a direction from order to chaos. Energy, while remaining constant in quantity, moves to lower potential and is less available to do work.

Applying this law to the origin of the universe, we reason that if the universe has had no beginning but is infinitely old, then it should have reached a state of complete disorder, with no available energy. If the universe were infinitely old it would have already died the heat death predicted by astronomy. Since we see order in the galaxies, order in the solar system, order on the Earth, and everywhere energy at a high potential, it must follow that the universe is not infinitely old. It had a beginning.

But it also follows from the first law that it could not create itself, and so must have been made by Something outside of the universe – a Creator.

Law of Cause and Effect

The law of cause and effect states that every effect must have a cause. It also states that the effect cannot be greater, in size or in kind, than the cause. This law follows directly from the first law of thermodynamics, and is also embodied in Newton's laws of motion. No exceptions to the law of cause and effect have ever been observed. It follows that every effect we see in the universe must have had a cause, and we can trace all effects back to a First Cause.

The First Cause of time must be greater than time, in fact eternal. The First Cause had no origin. This answers those who ask where God came from.

Space stretches beyond the limits of detection, so the First Cause of all this space must be greater than this, namely infinite. There can be no place free from the influence of the First Cause of space.

The universe contains a lot of energy, as we have already observed. There is the radiant energy of our sun, and of all the countless other stars. There is also the gravitational attraction between our sun and the planets of our solar system. This, though considerable on a human scale, is puny compared with the gravitational pull of stars in a galaxy, or yet again, between galaxies within clusters. The First Cause of all the energy in the universe cannot be less than the sum total of that energy, according to the law of cause and effect. That First Cause is omnipotent.

By similar logic, we can consider all the information; not just the intrinsic properties of matter, but the genetic information in all the varied forms of animal and vegetable life, and conclude that the First Cause must be omniscient – all-knowing.

We humans have personality and will. In order to create personalities, the First Cause must itself have a personality. A First Cause without a personality could not create personalities. The effect is not greater than the cause. We, as personalities, are interested in other personalities, and it is not unreasonable therefore to suppose that the First Cause created us so that He (a personal Creator), could have fellowship with us, and we with Him. The atheistic evolutionist ignores the spiritual aspect of both this life and the next.

Our sense of right and wrong, in personal life, in judicial systems and in games, might lead us to suppose that this First Cause is a righteous God. However, to go any further we must look for revelation, and possibly the experiences of others. The Bible has been found to be accurate in its science as well as its history, and there are millions of Christians who bear personal testimony to its reliability in pointing the way to fellowship with the First Cause – the eternal, infinite, omnipotent, all-wise, righteous and merciful God.

The Second Law and Evolution

The second law of thermodynamics says that in a closed system spontaneous processes lead to a decrease in order and organization. Evolution, on the other hand, is supposed to move onwards and upwards from particles to molecules to simple life and finally arrive at man whose brain is the most complex, organized material in the universe. Evolution, then, involves belief in a massive increase in order and organization, requiring a willing suspension of belief in the second law by evolutionists. Moreover, evolution is said to result from chance changes and natural selection, with no input of more information. Hence it can be seen that the theory of

Fair play.

evolution is directly at odds with this second law of thermo-dynamics which categorically states that things naturally move from order to disorder.

The Big Bang theory of the start of the universe violates the first law by creating matter and energy out of nothing. It then violates the second law by creating an ordered universe from an explosion. Explosions do not produce order, but chaos. The proposed Big Bang would have been a destructive event of unimaginable proportions, which could not have produced an ordered universe.

Of course, it is possible to increase order locally and temporarily. We see it every day in open systems where directed energy is applied. On a building site, materials are assembled. Much energy is expended, and the architect's plans are followed to assemble the building. The building has more order than its constituent parts, but the process is far from spontaneous. Energy and information are invested in the materials. Similarly an acorn grows into an oak tree with an increase in organization. Nutrients, water and sunlight are contributing to the open system, and the genetic information in the seed directs these to increase order. (Needless to say, building and oak tree alike will eventually spontaneously decay.)

The Third Law

Darwin imagined that sunlight and electric discharges would suffice to produce the first living cell in some warm pond of primaeval soup. But energy and chance will not increase order. The third law of thermodynamics says that order is at a maximum at absolute zero temperature. Adding raw energy (by raising the temperature) reduces the order. Raw energy added to an open system is not a recipe for increased organization. A bull in a china shop puts in energy, to produce chaos! Our examples above, of the building site and the acorn, both show that what is needed is directed energy – energy harnessed by information. Primaeval soup contains

A bull in a china shop puts energy in to produce chaos.

no information, so the third law rules it out as the precursor of life.

The fact that the second law of thermodynamics applies to a closed system does not remove the evolutionist's dilemma. In order to increase organization, an open system requires an input, not simply of energy, but of directed energy; energy plus information.

Logos

Creation involves an input of directed energy. The First Cause created time (the beginning), space (the heavens), and matter (the Earth), according to the first verse of the Bible. The Earth was formless and empty and the first chapter of Genesis goes on to describe an input of energy and information to increase the organization. Jeremiah (10 v 12) speaks of this input of energy and information. *'He hath made the earth by His power, He hath established the world by His wisdom, and hath stretched out the heavens by His discretion.'* And the first chapter of John's gospel refers to the Creator as the 'Word' (Greek: Logos = information).

Incidentally, the more power and wisdom a worker has at his disposal, the quicker the job will be done and the better will be the result. An omnipotent and omniscient First Cause would create things instantaneously, and to perfection. Psalm 33 says He spoke and it was done. And Genesis reports that it was good.

As applied to information theory, the second law says that chance changes result in a loss of information; a decrease in signal to noise ratio. Biological mutations have long been considered the source of new genetic information for natural selection to use in evolving 'higher' forms of life. But mutations are chance changes in the genes, and by this law must lead to a loss of information. No beneficial mutation has ever been reported, and most mutations are clearly deleterious. Hornless cattle are beneficial to the rancher rather than the cattle, and pipless oranges are helpful to the consumer rather than to the orange!

28

Order cannot come from an explosion.

Information theory tells us that information can only arise by an input from an intelligent source. Genetic information required a Logos. Chance is clearly the opposite of design, and mutations the reverse of information.

The idea is put about that evolution theory is the scientific view of origins, while creationism is an abuse of science. We have considered fundamental laws observed to hold in all circumstances. Creation is in harmony with those laws while evolution theory runs counter to them.

Origin of Consistent Laws

It is instructive to consider why scientific laws are unchanging. The creationist sees them as the expression of an unchanging Creator who has revealed Himself as the same yesterday, today and forever. To the evolutionist who sees everything resulting from chance, the reason for this consistency is a mystery. Inexplicably, matter and energy, called into being by chance and organized by random events, are yet subject to immutable laws. The very existence of laws points to a faithful Creator. *'I am the Lord. I change not'*.

Chapter 3

The Big Bang Theory Exploded

The atheists not only need an explanation of how living things came into being and then diversified, they also need to explain how the matter in the universe was formed. The explanation most recently in favour was the so-called big bang, an explosion which threw all the clusters of galaxies into space. While some Christian apologists were happy to accept this explanation (John Polkinghorne, among others), many scientists are now discarding this scenario. The scientific literature recently contained comments such as this which was printed in Nature on 10th August 1989; 'Apart from being philosophically unacceptable, the Big Bang is an over-simple view of how the universe began, and is unlikely to survive the decade ahead... In all respects save that of convenience, this view of the origin of the universe is thoroughly unsatisfactory. It is an effect whose cause cannot be identified, or even discussed.'

Red-Shift

When atoms are excited, their electrons jump to higher energy levels, and in returning to their ground state emit light of particular frequencies. These spectral lines can be recognized by their position and pattern as being due to a particular element. However, when astronomers observe the same patterns of lines in distant starlight, they find that the lines have been red-shifted. That is, each line has a frequency that is lower than the corresponding line as seen on earth. This red-shift (red is the low frequency colour in the visible spectrum) is attributed to movement of the star away from the earth. (This apparent Doppler Effect would be analogous to the shift to lower frequencies of the sounds emitted by an ambulance as it passes an observer and speeds away.) The galaxies with the greater red-shifts are assumed to be at a greater distance from the earth, and to be moving away from the earth faster. By this theory, it seems to us that everything beyond our own solar system is moving away from us, and that the more distant objects are retreating more rapidly. The picture emerges of a universe in which everything is moving apart from everything else, as in the aftermath of a gigantic explosion. If one could run the picture back for some 15 billion years, all the matter in the universe would have been together in one small volume. Depending on the initial velocity with which the universe was thrown apart, it would either continue to expand indefinitely, or the rate of expansion would slow down and stop. Gravity would then reverse the process until everything collapsed in upon itself once more. Such a cycle could conceivably be repeated endlessly.

The observed background radiation of 2.8 degrees Kelvin (2.8 degrees C above absolute zero temperature) was said to be the residual energy from that alleged explosion. Such a vestige of the explosion of an initial hot, dense, cosmic egg was predicted in the 1940s and discovered in the mid sixties.

With red-shift and background radiation energy both supporting the big bang theory for the origin of the universe, why did scientists become unhappy with this model?

Free Meal?

Firstly one has to ask how the material of the universe arose in the first place. The first law of thermodynamics says that matter and energy cannot be created or destroyed. A theory has been advanced that, given the first few kilograms of matter, the rest could produce itself by a process of self-creation. Apparently this 'free meal' idea can be tolerated because, for such a unique situation, perhaps we should not expect the normal laws of physics to be obeyed!

Order from an Explosion?

Secondly, all observed explosions are destructive, leading to a chaotic condition. My own research in synthetic chemistry with acetylenic compounds (from behind an explosion screen), frequently left me sweeping up powdered glass which had once been apparatus. Sadly, terrorist car-bombs have shown us the destructive power of explosions. The postulated big bang would have been the ultimate in destructive incidents. Yet we see the universe with its ordered spiral galaxies, and within our solar system the degree of order is breath-taking. The ancients looked for the rising of the star Sirius over the Nile at dawn, knowing that this would be repeated 365 days, 6 hours, 9 minutes and 9.6 seconds later – a sidereal year. Such is the order in the solar system that we can send space-probes on predetermined paths. Everywhere in the universe we see order and available energy. This is not what we would expect as the outcome of an explosion.

Cause of Red-Shift?

Thirdly, we cannot be sure that the red-shift is due to the Doppler Effect in an expanding universe. For example, in the journal New Scientist in November 1989 it was reported; 'Unusual effects in which light is scattered might be causing large shifts in the wavelengths of light in the optical spectra of distant galaxies and quasars. This could mimic the effects of the expansion of the universe, which astronomers believe causes the light in distant objects to be red-shifted.' Of even greater interest to a creationist whose biblical world-view spans a mere six thousand years of history, the Russian scientist, V.S. Troitskii, of the Radiophysical Research Institute, Gorky, has suggested (Astrophysics and Space Science, vol 139, (1987) 389–411), that the red-shift is due to a decreasing speed at which light travels. He suggests that the universe is in fact contracting. He concludes that a decrease in the velocity of light would give a satisfactory explanation of two otherwise puzzling phenomena. Within very distant galaxies, objects are sometimes observed to be moving relative to one another at speeds many times greater than the presently observed speed of light. This would only be possible if we were seeing the galaxy as it was when light had a much greater velocity. Also explained by a decreasing speed of light would be the observation that the 2.8 K background radiation is the same all over the universe. Troitskii commented in his paper that if his idea were correct, the universe must be very much younger than we had thought. (We shall return to the subject of the speed of light in a later chapter.)

Background Radiation

The fourth reason why scientists generally are unhappy with the big bang hypothesis is that in every direction in which it has been measured, the background radiation is found to have the same value. In 1989 astronomers discovered walls of clusters of galaxies stretching from horizon to horizon over the North. This 'Great Wall', estimated to be some five thousand billion billion kilometres long, is the largest structure ever seen. Other parts of the universe are vast empty spaces. Theory cannot explain how this anisotropy, or lumpiness, could result from the big bang. Also the lumpiness should be reflected in a similar anisotropy of background radiation. As New Scientist put it in April, 1990; '...many accepted theories of galaxy formation will have to go if the data build up and continue to show there is no variation in the background radiation. Galaxies could only have condensed from the stuff of the big bang, if it was lumpy ... big bang theories will be in a lot of trouble.'

On the 3rd January, 1991, the scientific journal Nature carried a report on the work of a group of scientists who had been mapping our bit of the universe (the nearest 450 million light years). The map showed vast empty spaces as well as networks of clusters and superclusters of galaxies. Yet studies of the background radiation using NASA's Cosmic Background Explorer (Cobe) satellite show that the radiation is extremely smooth and entirely uniform in all directions. The radiation simply cannot be the echo of the proposed big bang. One of the scientists, Dr Will Saunders of Oxford University, said 'We are now left without a single best-buy theory, for the first time in a decade, to explain the whole of cosmology.' The Cold Dark Matter hypothesis fails to account for the superclusters, and the big bang has become a damp squib!

Age of Universe?

The age of the universe was obtained from the time it would have taken for an expansion from the proposed initial cosmic egg to today's situation. When the big bang theory was first postulated, it did not find favour (over the then current steady state hypothesis) because it gave an age for the universe lower than that accepted for the evolution of life on earth. With the big bang theory now rejected, the journal New Scientist suggested in March 1991 that the red-shift had nothing to do with distance. This throws the subject of the age of the universe back into the melting pot. Science advances by such adjustments to theory, and the history of science is littered with discarded ideas. Evolutionists judge the age of the universe by the time that they think is required to produce the living world. They automatically rule out a cosmos created complete some six thousand years ago by an all-powerful, all-wise God. Such a biblical world-view is then called unscientific by those whose 'scientific' theories are continually having to be discarded!

The stars in their courses.

Chapter 4

Primaeval Soup

No one now believes that moth grubs can arise spontaneously from old clothes, or frogs from marshland. This sort of belief persisted from ancient times until the careful work of Pasteur in the nineteenth century. However, if life cannot arise without a living Creator, we must all perforce be creationists. It is not surprising then, that the modern theory of how life arose by chance was proposed by two atheists, Oparin of the USSR and Haldane, of Britain.

In the 1920s, it was possible to imagine that the first single-celled life-form was fairly simple. But with the growth of our understanding of biochemistry since the fifties, we can now see that the 'protozoon' is of incredible complexity.

The Miller Experiment

In 1953 the American chemist Miller passed 60,000 volt discharges through a boiling mixture of water, methane, hydrogen and ammonia (a reducing atmosphere). The product was a tarry goo which tended to decompose in the highly energetic circumstances under which it was made. Miller used a cold-trap in his apparatus to isolate products from the destructive influence of the conditions of the experiment. From the goo he was able to separate the simplest amino acids, glycine and alanine. The more complex amino acids

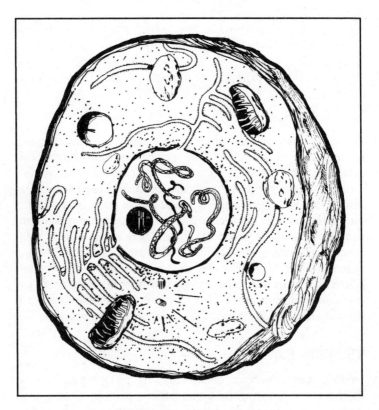

The complexity of a 'simple' cell.

necessary to form proteins have not been made in this way. Further, some amino acids not found at all in proteins turned up in these experiments. These results were excitedly hailed as evidence for abiogenesis (beginning without life). Other workers tried variations to obtain other simple molecules called the building blocks of life.

Needless to say, these gooey mixtures of a few simple amino acids fall a very long way short of the simplest protein, which in turn is much further still from the simplest living cell, with its thousands of different complex enzymes and nucleic acids all operating in concert.

Selection of L Amino Acids and D Sugars

All amino acids except glycine have an asymmetric carbon atom which allows them to exist in two optically active forms, one L or left-handed and the other D or right-handed. When made in the laboratory from non-optically active starting materials, the amino acids are racemic mixtures containing equal amounts of left and right handed forms. This is because left and right handed forms have an equal probability of being formed. In nature, only the L forms are found. Hence such laboratory experiments are not able to duplicate the supposed origin of life. The fact that in living things the amino acids are all left-handed gives to strings of them (proteins) a three dimensional structure (helical or pleated) whose shape is vital to their function. The probability of even a short string of amino acids being all left handed is vanishingly small.

In a similar way, sugars found in carbohydrates and nucleic acids have asymmetric carbon atoms, but with sugars all forms in nature are D isomers. Chemists have been unable to account for this selectivity. Sugars combine with bases and phosphoric acid to produce a string of nucleic acid. (Nucleic acids are DNA and RNA which carry the genetic information.) These constituents can combine in a number of different ways, over and above the particular configuration always found in life-forms. Again, because laboratory

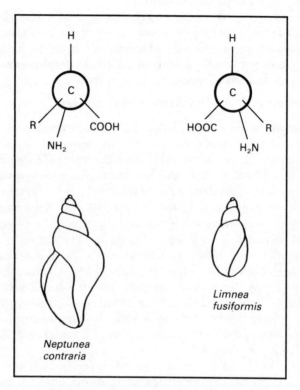

Right- and left-handedness in amino acids and shells.

experiments give mixtures of products, there is no way that such studies can reflect what might have happened in some primaeval soup to produce the first life.

The Oxygen Problem

Organic biomolecules such as proteins, which are constituents of all life, are sensitive to oxygen, and are decomposed in air. The atmosphere that Urey and Miller had proposed for the origin of life, perhaps a couple of thousand million years ago (all the best make-believe stories begin 'Once upon a time...') had to be free of oxygen. Geologists have objected because the 'earliest' rocks contain iron in its red oxidized form, and carbonate, both difficult to account for in a reducing environment with no oxygen.

Nucleic acids are very sensitive to ultra violet radiation, which rapidly destroys them. If the early atmosphere contained oxygen, this would destroy the proteins. However, if the early atmosphere contained no oxygen then it would also be devoid of ozone, a form of oxygen. Without a protective ozone layer high in the atmosphere, the uv content of sunlight would destroy the nucleic acids. If oxygen were present the components of a living cell could not be formed, but if oxygen were absent the components of a living cell still could not be formed. Only a living cell created complete and fully formed is capable of surviving, functioning and reproducing itself.

The Chicken and Egg Problem

Within a cell, the nucleic acids code for the making of the enzymes and the enzymes manufacture the nucleic acids, all with incredible speed and precision. The first cell must have required not only the nucleic acids, but also the different enzymes which work in concert to make the DNA. 'There is a hitch' reports Scientific American in an article in its February 1991 issue, which surveys a number of recent theories of how life began. 'Proteins cannot form without DNA, but neither can DNA form without proteins. To those pondering the origin of life, it is a classic chicken-and-egg problem. Which came first, proteins or DNA?' On a number of counts, it is clear that the primaeval soup theory, proposed in the name of science, is no more scientific than the pre-Pasteur ideas of the spontaneous generation of lice in old socks.

Origin of Genetic Information

The Nucleic acids (DNA, RNA, mRNA, tRNA) carry the genetic information of the life form by virtue of the order of their different base components. Thus, just as a series of dots and dashes, in a particular sequence, can be translated using the Morse code, so the order of four bases on the string of a nucleic acid will code for the manufacture of the various enzymes (proteins) in the cell. The order has to be precise. This requires design. The code is information. This requires intelligence. Nucleic acids cannot be the product of chance.

The information in living things is the most clearly indisputable evidence for a Creator. According to Norbert Wiener, the founder of cybernetics and information theory, information cannot be of a physical nature, even though it is transmitted by physical means. 'Information is information, neither matter nor energy. No materialism that fails to take account of this can survive the present day.'

Miller's experiments forty years ago had raised such hopes that the possibility of a materialistic origin of life had been demonstrated. In the article in Scientific American referred to above, Stanley Miller is quoted as saying 'The problem of the origin of life has turned out to be much more difficult than I, and most other people, imagined'. Miller was asked 'Do you ever entertain the possibility that genesis was a miracle not reproducible by humans?' 'Not at all' he replied, 'I think we just haven't learned the right tricks yet.'

To give an idea of just how efficient the DNA molecule

can be as a carrier of information, Professor Werner Gitt, Head of Data Processing at the Federal Institute of Physics and Technology, Braunschweig, Germany, has compared the information density of DNA with that of the megachip. If all the knowledge currently stored in the world's libraries could be stored on DNA molecules, 1% of the volume of a pinhead would be sufficient for this purpose. If, on the other hand, this information were to be stored with the aid of megachips, we would need a pile higher than the distance between the earth and the moon. The DNA is 45 million million times more efficient than man's hi-tech silicon devices. Stanley L. Miller was right in saying that man has not learned the right tricks yet!

DNA and Little Green Men

In 1990 the Hubble Telescope was launched into orbit and began to send back pictures to earth from space. One of the declared aims of the project was to look for other planets outside our Solar system, and to try to find extra-terrestrial life. How are we to recognize signs of life? We must look for coded messages by scanning the sky at various frequencies to try to pick up intelligent signals. The signals would have a non-random sequence (a design) and would carry information. Design and information are recognized as the product of intelligent life. Yet here on earth we look at the simplest cell, with its incredibly miniaturised design and information, and wonder if it could somehow have arisen by chance! The reason for this double standard is that scientists, like other mortals, look for evidence which will support their philosophical world-view. If life has evolved on earth by chance, then surely it has evolved in many other places in this vast universe. While it is recognized that intelligent life-forms would send non-random messages, it is not accepted that non-random sequences in genetic material here on earth can only be the product of an intelligent Designer. Evolutionism is not so much a science, more a philosophical world-view, with all the dogmatic assertions of a religion.

Splashes or Brushstrokes

When we come to admire some modern paintings, where the artist has sought an effect by splashing colour around the canvas and then riding a bicycle over it, we might mistakenly imagine that the masterpiece was the result of chance. With a painting of the Cubist school, we see geometric shapes in varied hues. There is much more evidence of design. Such careful brush-work could not have happened by chance. With a portrait or landscape there is also careful brushwork. Moreover there is information in the picture to show us that there was an intelligent designer. If we compare this with the case of the simplest living form, we see here also not only design but information. We are forced to conclude that an Intelligence designed the living cell, and that chance could not achieve its formation, even given billions of years.

Chapter 5

The Diversity of Life

We have seen that life could not have arisen by chance. Cells are immensely complicated. There is absolutely no possibility that a complete cell could just arrive by chance. Until a first cell was complete its components would be highly unstable. Nor would there have been a biological machine to aid its assembly. Natural selection could not be an on-going process until the cell could reproduce itself. Imagine a computer assembling itself by chance! The simplest cell is many orders of magnitude more complex than the most advanced computer (and much smaller). Imagine a computer, with the ability to collect and assemble another computer just like itself from raw materials from which it manufactured components, and imagine such a computer just happening by chance! Small wonder that Hoyle and Wickramasinghe, both confirmed evolutionists, were arguing in the 1970s that there must be an Intelligence behind the Universe.

However, if evolutionists can convince themselves that life first arose by chance, their difficulties are only just beginning. How did the proposed first cell develop and diversify into invertebrates such as shell fish, then into fish, amphibians, reptiles and on to birds and mammals, culminating in mankind?

An Ancient Lie

The idea of such a progression goes back to the ancient Babylonians, and Aristotle the Greek taught that we developed from fish. The French biologist Lamarck, at the beginning of the nineteenth century, suggested that acquired characteristics could be inherited. The giraffe, by stretching up to the leaves on the higher branches of trees might conceivably have developed a long neck. How the shorter female and juvenile giraffes survived is not clear! But would the giraffe's offspring have inherited its longer neck? The weight-lifter's arms become muscular with the practice of his sport, but this development does not effect his genes. His children are not born with bigger muscles. Lamarck's ideas are no longer accepted and in evolutionist circles today, Lamarckian is almost as great a term of abuse as Creationist is.

Darwinism

Charles Darwin, half a century later, suggested that since there were small variations within kinds of animals and plants, some varieties might have greater survival value than others. Varieties of the 'fitter' types would proliferate, and a changing environment would select the fittest from these. All this would occur gradually over vast periods of time. Hutton had already given Darwin such time by his interpretation of the rate of build up of sedimentary rocks. The supposed geological ages offer the time scale required for the alleged evolution of life.

By the middle of the twentieth century it was realized that natural selection can no more provide endless change than can the directed selection practised by breeders. Dogs can be bred to give smaller and smaller animals, but they never become anything other than canine. (In the absence of breeders, dogs interbreed and revert to the fitter mongrel type.) With increasing selection the poor dogs become less healthy, as some traits are bred out. The pedigree dog has a less rich gene pool than the mongrel. In the same way, wheat

Giraffes necks were not lengthened by stretching up.

can be selected to give increased yields and shorter stalks, but the grain falls prey to disease. Nor is it ever anything but wheat.

Far from being a mechanism for change, it is clear that natural selection is a conserving influence. Consider how natural selection would treat an incipient wing in a reptile which was about to evolve into a bird. Until fully formed and functioning, such a partial wing would be an encumbrance. It would be eliminated by natural selection since the proto-bird would be less fit to survive with it.

Neo-Darwinism

The 'Neo-Darwinian Synthesis' proclaimed that mutations to the genetic material would provide the new information for natural selection to work on. A problem for the neo-darwinian is that mutations, brought on most readily by high energy radiation or by carcinogenic chemicals, always leave the life-form less fit. The mutant fan-tailed gold-fish does not live as long as unmutated (unmutilated!) varieties. Mutations are almost always damaging and sometimes lethal. No entirely beneficial mutation has been recorded.

Bio-systems have proof-reading mechanisms to prevent mistakes in copying genetic information, so mutations are rare events in nature. Mutations have been studied most intently and for almost a century in the fruit fly Drosophila. With its short life span, thirty generations can be bred in a year. Irradiated flies show damage to eyes and wings, but no super-flies were bred, and nothing beyond a fly has ever evolved from these concentrated experiments.

Genetic information is precise. Chance mutations must be deleterious because they lead to a loss of information. It is a bit like changing the electrical connections inside a complex computer in the hope of improving its functioning power. The philosophical premise that life developed by chance has led to the nonsensical conclusion that man is the product of a very protracted series of mistakes in the copying of genes of a protozoon.

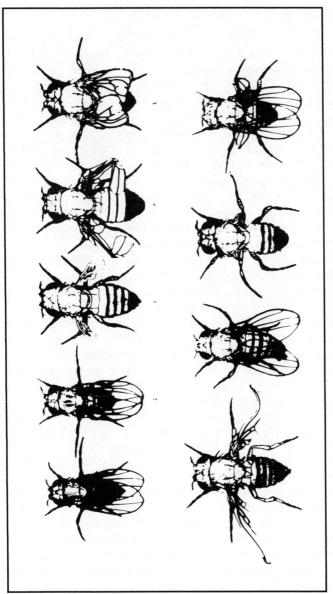

Irradiated fruit flies.

Evolution at the Molecular Level

A further problem with this theory of chance changes selected by the environment follows from the fact that genetic information is so precise. The genetic information for a reptile is such that it produces a creature exquisitely suited to its habitat in all particulars. The same can be said concerning the bird. Yet the reptile is supposed to have evolved into the bird, according to their relative positions in the fossil record. If the reptile did indeed evolve into the bird, then every small mutation must have been selected because it was an improvement on this exquisite design. There must have been a progression of creatures gradually changing from reptile to bird, each better adapted to the presumed changing conditions than its immediate ancestors. The metabolisms of cold-blooded reptiles and warm-blooded birds are very different. The biomolecules of their body cells must also gradually change. Yet these are precisely shaped molecules whose functions depend on their shapes, which in turn are derived from an exact sequence of components. When it is considered that a change of one amino acid in the sequence of components in human haemoglobin produces a collapse of the blood cell to give sickle cell anaemia, one can see how impossible it would be to get a long series of small changes, each facilitating the grand march forward of evolution.

Missing Links

If evolution had proceeded by a series of small progressions over millions of years, one would expect that there would be more intermediate forms than static classes of life forms. Today we do not find any intermediate forms at all. There are no incipient organs and no vestigial parts. In the fossil record we do not find these intermediates. In fact they are known as 'missing links'. The importance of the archaeopteryx fossils lies in the claim that it is a link between reptiles and birds. Heavy bones and the lack of a large sternum mean

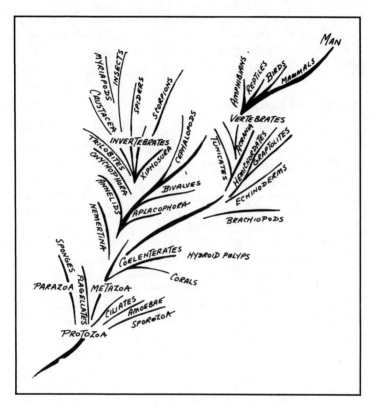

From Sir Gavin de Beer's 'Atlas' – still imaginary,
but 'tree' is not joined together.

that the archaeopteryx was probably a flightless bird. Such birds exist today. It had claws on its wings, but so does the juvenile hoatzin bird today. It had teeth. Other extinct birds had teeth. Not all reptiles have teeth, nor all mammals. The feathers on these fossils were perfectly formed. Archaeopteryx was a bird, not an intermediate. Incidentally, a fossil called Proavis, very much like a modern bird, has been found at lower levels in the geological strata than archaeopteryx, so this rules out 'Archy' as the forerunner of birds.

Punctuated Equilibria

That archaeopteryx is the best example of a 'missing link' is an indication of the paucity of the evidence from the fossil record. Indeed, it is so meagre that two leading evolutionists in America suggested that evolution does not take place gradually at all. The 'Punctuated Equilibria' theory of Eldredge and Gould supposed that in small isolated communities, rapid changes occurred (fast in terms of the alleged billions of years of geology). Because these changes happened so quickly in small groups, they left no fossil record. Long periods of equilibrium when no changes occurred were apparently punctuated by short bursts of major changes. All this was conjectured because of the negative evidence of lack of fossil intermediates. Gould has since (1990) introduced yet another theory to explain the mechanism of evolution, based on the rich variety of forms in the Burgess Shales. In the new theory, chance is the arbiter of change and natural selection plays little or no part. Incidentally, there are at least fifteen modern theories of evolution. If any one of them were satisfactory there would only be that one.

Evolution and Increasing Complexity

We have said that the single celled life form is unimaginably complex. However, man's brain is thought to be the most highly ordered material in the Universe. Evolution of life

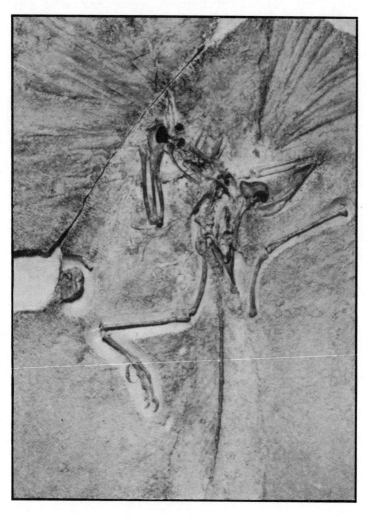

The fossil Archaeopteryx.

forms from the single cell to man must involve an increasing complexity. Chance and time are said to accomplish this. Evolution, with its inherent claim of ever increasing complexity of kinds, could not have happened spontaneously. No amount of energy added to the open system can achieve this. It would require an input of information from a Designer. (But the Designer told us that He created things after their kind with their seed within themselves.) Much ingenuity has been expended in trying to get round the problem of spontaneously increasing complexity. People have used computers to generate non-randomness. Carefully designed programs have been run in order to show that order can arise without an input of information! Where a system is well away from equilibrium, of course, random changes may produce temporary increases in order, but such progress is haphazard and cannot be sustained.

No Agreed Mechanism

It would seem that there is no general consensus amongst evolutionists as to the mechanism of evolution. There is not even a theoretically possible mechanism for change. On the contrary, evolution runs counter to the laws of thermodynamics. Yet evolution is widely regarded as the scientific model, whilst creationists are seen as unscientific. Evolution theory also proposes the opposite view to the account in Genesis chapter one. How sad that many church leaders choose to put their faith in evolution when considering the origin of man.

Chapter 6

Molecular Biology Refutes Evolution

We have referred to the search for a mechanism for evolution in biological systems. We have seen that natural selection produces no new genetic information. We saw that mutations are destructive rather than creative. The branch of biology which has seen the greatest advances in our knowledge during the second half of the twentieth century is molecular biology. Genes express the structure of a plant or animal, so the secret of evolution, if it has taken place, should be found in the genetic molecules and the proteins they code for.

In 1985 the molecular biologist Michael Denton produced a book about evolution. It was significant because Dr Denton is not a creationist and has made no claim to follow the Christian faith. His book, entitled 'Evolution – a theory in crisis', is a devastating indictment of evolution theory from his own special field. We shall summarize some of the points he makes.

No Organisms Ancestral

All self-sufficient organisms are composed of a cell or a number of cells. The eukaryotic cell has within the cell wall a nucleus containing the nucleic acids which carry genetic information for the organism. Also within the cell wall but outside of the nucleus are found a number of other structures. Here are found several thousand different bio-molecules, each of which performs a specific task. Examples of these would be cytochrome C which converts carbohydrate into energy, hormones which regulate growth, and haemoglobin which transfers oxygen to myoglobin in the muscles while removing carbon dioxide and water. The interesting aspect for our present consideration is that all organisms, from the simplest to the most complex, contain the same bio-molecules. Haemoglobin in a sea squirt is not, of course, identical to haemoglobin in a cat. A cat breathes in oxygen at one fifth atmospheric pressure while the sea squirt extracts its oxygen from water at a much lower partial pressure. (Heme in the cat, as with ourselves, is an iron porphin, while in the squirt the metal is vanadium. Evolution of the blood would not only require changes in the protein of the haemoglobin, but also the transmutation of the metal in any imagined evolution of this sea creature to a land mammal.)

If all creatures contain in their body cells the same kinds of molecules, we cannot say that the simpler types are more primitive, nor yet ancestral. The slug contains bio-molecules which are every bit as complex as their counterpart in man. Man, as a complete organism, is of course more complex, but at a molecular level, the slug is his equal!

Biomolecules cannot Evolve

Evolution of these precisely engineered molecules would be impossible because even small changes in their chemical make-up impair or destroy their ability to function. Enzymes, which promote or inhibit chemical reactions in the cells, work by a lock-and-key mechanism whereby their shape exactly fits that of a substrate. If the shape of the 'lock' were to evolve, it would require the shape of the 'key' to evolve in a matching pattern – a chemical impossibility.

So not only is no organism ancestral to any other kind, but there is no theoretical route for bio-molecules to evolve from those in one kind of living thing to those in another. Denton says; 'Each class at a molecular level is unique, isolated and unlinked by intermediates. Thus molecules, like fossils have failed to provide the elusive intermediates so long sought by evolutionary biology. Again, the only relationships identified by this new technique are sisterly. At a molecular level, no organism is 'ancestral' or 'primitive' or 'advanced' compared with its relatives. Nature seems to conform to the same non-evolutionary and intensely circumferential pattern that was long ago perceived by the great comparative anatomists of the nineteenth century.' Denton goes on to say; 'There is little doubt that if this molecular evidence had been available one century ago it would have been seized upon with devastating effect by the opponents of evolution theory like Agassiz and Owen, and the idea of organic evolution might never have been accepted.'

Paley's Watchmaker

The complexity of bio-molecules makes them islands of viability separated from each other by unbridgeable gaps. Since they could not have evolved and since they are so complex, we can confidently say that they must have been designed by an Intelligence. This argument was originally used by William Paley about whole organisms, but was considered flawed when it was thought that natural selection could produce a perfect living thing. Used of bio-molecules, only the most doctrinaire believer in atheistic evolution would try to refute this truism.

Amino Acid Sequences Compared

We noted that haemoglobin in sea squirts is slightly different from that in cats, because each is precisely tailored for the habitat of the particular creature. (We have seen that it is not, as Lamarck suggested, tailored by the habitat.) Techniques are now available for determining the exact sequence of amino acids in proteins such as the globin of haemoglobin. Hence one can calculate percentage sequence differences in order to see which forms are closely related. It was hoped that this technique would enable scientists to build an evolutionary tree in which creatures with small sequence differences would be on the same branches, and that evolutionary relationships would be proved. Tables of differences in the order of amino acids are published (the Dayhoff 'Atlas of Protein Sequence and Structure', 1972) and Denton uses the data to show that evolutionary relationships do not exist.

The figure shows one of several sets of sequence differences used in Denton's book to show that, far from indicating an evolutionary relationship, sequence differences show that biochemically the kinds are separate and distinct. The lamprey is a jawless eel thought by evolutionists to be a fore-runner of true fish. But the difference in the order of amino acids in the haemoglobins of lamprey and carp, a fish, is 75%. Almost exactly the same percentage differences separate the haemoglobins of lamprey and frog, an amphibian; lamprey and chicken, a bird; lamprey and kangaroo and lamprey and human. As 1 Corinthians 15 says; *'All flesh is not the same flesh: but there is one kind of flesh of men, another flesh of beasts, another of fishes, and another of birds.'* Perhaps if Paul had been a modern day molecular biologist instead of a tent maker, he might have added 'and another of jawless eels'!

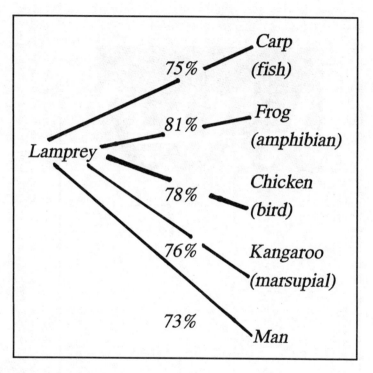

Amino acid sequence differences in haemoglobins.

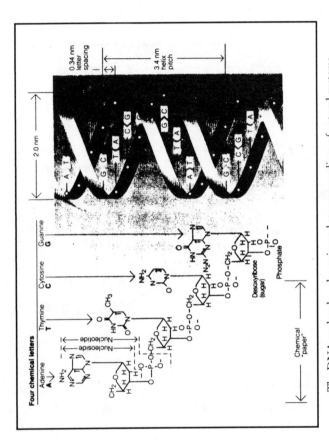

The DNA molecule – the universal storage medium of natural systems.
A short section of a strand of the double helix with sugar–phosphate chain reveals its chemical structure (left).
The schematic representation of the double helix (right) shows the base pairs coupled by hydrogen bridges
(in a plane perpendicular to the helical axis).

Chapter 7

Genetics and Creation

'Like father, like son' is a saying which reflects the observation that offspring resemble parents. Plants and animals reproduce after their kind, with their seed within themselves. However a son is not an exact clone of his father, since he inherits characteristics from both parents, as well as from grandparents. Mendel's experiments in the middle of the 19th century showed that a seed contained 'factors' (we call them genes) which control the expression of characteristics.

Chemicals and Information

Today we know that genetic material is carried on the DNA molecule, a string of nucleotides, each composed of a sugar, a phosphate group and a base. The nucleotides of DNA differ only in their bases, which can be one of four molecules. The DNA string is rather like a sequence of dots and dashes in a Morse code message. It carries genetic information which enables the characteristics of the organism to be expressed. DNA molecules range from a few thousand to many millions of nucleotide pairs on a double strand, one strand being complementary to the other.

The sequence of the nucleotides in the DNA codes for the organization of amino acids in proteins. Three adjacent nucleotides specify for a particular amino acid. Most of the

61

20 amino acids found in proteins can be specified by more than one sequence of three nucleotides, since there are 64 possible ways of arranging the four different nucleotides into groups of three.

Genes and Chromosomes

A length of DNA which expresses a characteristic is found in a gene, and many genes together are packaged in chromosomes. A gene may be involved in the expression of more than one characteristic, and more than one gene may be responsible for the expression of a single characteristic. (Two genes code for eye colour in humans.)

Man has 46 chromosomes, composed of 23 pairs. All cells in the human body have these 46 chromosomes, except sperm and egg cells which have only 23. A fertilized egg then has its complement of 46 chromosomes inherited from both parents. This provides for variety in physical characteristics. To code for these, the DNA consists of about three thousand million nucleotide pairs in double strands.

Variation

Variation produced in offspring, by different combinations of parental genes, cannot produce anything novel, any more than the shuffling of a pack of cards could produce an eleven of hearts! Variations within a kind should not be confused with evolution, although it is often referred to misleadingly as micro-evolution. For example, changes in melanism in the population of the speckled moth, biston betularia, due to changes in the environment, have nothing to do with evolution. From start to finish, the population contained both light and dark forms of this species of moth, and they were never anything other than biston betularia.

Do Genes Evolve?

In order for an organism to evolve into something other than what it is, new genetic information must be provided. This

Melanism in peppered moths, *Biston betularia.*

would require the changing of existing genetic information, or the addition of new information.

When cells divide to reproduce themselves, there is a high degree of fidelity in the duplication of the information in the genes. The making of a nucleotide (which would take a trained chemist with sophisticated apparatus days to perform) occurs in the cell during replication at the rate of 100 every second. It is estimated that mistakes in copying occur at a frequency of only one in a hundred thousand million nucleotides. Even then there are enzymes which repair incorrect or damaged nucleotides in order to eliminate mistakes in the copying process. This conserving machinery acts to prevent changes in the genes.

Mutations in Genetic Material

When changes do occur, as the result of mutagenic chemicals, radiation or mistakes in copying, the resultant mutant gene is usually incapable of functioning. Most mutations are harmful or lethal to the organism. A mistake in a precisely orchestrated machine is not likely to improve the functioning of the machine. No truly beneficial mutation has ever been recorded. (The mutation responsible for sickle-cell anaemia also renders its carrier immune to malaria. This is because the life-span of the defective blood cell is shorter than the incubation period of the malaria. It is not due to any improvement in the blood cell. In regions where malaria is a common cause of death, sickle-cell anaemia carriers do have a relative advantage, and a higher proportion of the population carry the mutant gene. So it would seem that this mutation could be beneficial where malaria is endemic. However, where the defective gene is inherited from both parents, the sufferer usually dies before reaching adulthood.)

The party game where a whispered message is passed round the room from mouth to ear demonstrates that mistakes in copying do corrupt information. Since changes in genetic information are deleterious, mutations in genetic material can hardly be the modus operandi of a proposed evolution.

Mutations of chromosomes do occur. These can involve a segment lost from a chromosome or the duplication of a segment so that the same segment occurs twice in a chromosome. Occasionally a segment of a chromosome may be reversed so that nucleotides occur in the wrong order. Translocation can also happen, where the position of a segment within a chromosome is changed. Segments on different chromosomes may become exchanged. Could these rare mistakes be a mechanism for evolution?

The segments of genetic information on the chromosomes are analogous to the pages in a book. From time to time in the production of a book, at the type-setting stage, a mistake is made – a mutation. Usually the mistake is noted and rectified by the proof reader – the repair enzymes. If the mistake gets through, it leads to a loss of information. At the binding stage of book production, very infrequently the pages are bound in the wrong order, or perhaps a couple of pages appear upside-down, or pages may be left out or even duplicated. These are akin to chromosomal mutations. The book is less functional as a carrier of information. No new information is introduced by such errors. Nor does the book evolve from fiction to non-fiction!

Transfer of Genes between Bacteria

It has been found that DNA segments, called episomes, may be transferred from one bacterial cell to another, becoming incorporated into the genetic make-up of the host. Such episomes contain genes which build bridges between bacterial cells in order to effect transfer. They may also contain genes which impart to the invaded bacterial cell a resistance to certain antibiotics. This is certainly a mechanism for increasing genetic information in a cell, so may it be regarded as a candidate for an evolutionary mechanism?

Two factors, however, should be noted in this regard.

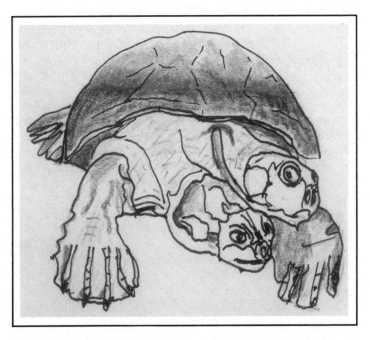

Two-headed mutant turtle.

Bacteria differ from cells of all plants and animals in that they have no membrane surrounding the genetic material. The bacterial cell has no nucleus. Invasion of exterior DNA into eukaryotic cells (cells containing a nucleus) has not been noted outside of the genetic engineering laboratory. The other factor of note is that the episome appears to be purpose-built for invading other bacterial cells and implanting information in them. Episomes cannot, by virtue of their information content, arise by chance. This mechanism is clearly part of the design of these life-forms. Unless the episome were perfectly formed it could not operate. To return to genetic engineering, this is a carefully designed operation to impart genetic information. As such it qualifies as creation rather than evolution.

Natural Selection

It has been claimed that natural selection plays a part in the alleged evolution of life-forms. A mutant which is more fitted to a change in the environment is favourably selected. However, since mutations range from inconsequential to catastrophic in their effect upon the viability of the individual, mutants are more likely to be weeded out by natural selection. Where a mutant gene is inherited from only one parent, the non-mutant allele can be expressed, but if the mutant gene is inherited from both parents, this leads to a loss of fitness. Thus the mutant would tend to be eliminated by natural selection.

Natural selection is, therefore, a conserving mechanism rather than a means of evolving kinds which are more fit.

Common Genetic Code

A particular sequence of three nucleotides always, as far as is known, codes for the same amino acid, whether in a spider or an elephant. The sequential information on the nucleic acid DNA in the genes is transferred to similar nucleic acids known as RNA. (Enzymes which carry out these transcriptions recognize initiator and terminator sequences on the DNA string.) Each sequence of three nucleotides on the m-RNA codes for a particular amino acid, so a string of thousands of nucleotides would code for a protein containing one third of that number of amino acids in an exact sequence. (The precise sequence of amino acids in proteins gives them their shape and active sites which enable the proteins to do their particular jobs, just as the exact shape of a key enables it to undo a lock.)

According to some geneticists, this seeming universality of the genetic code in all life-forms, from single celled bacteria to humans, is good corroborative evidence that evolution has occurred. This is not unassailable proof of evolution, even though one might expect that there would be a common code if all organisms had evolved from an original cell. An equally logical explanation for the common design for gene translation is that all organisms were created by the same Designer. In the field of engineering, for instance, different machines use the same basic patterns and principles.

Genetic Information

As already noted, this transcription mechanism is rather like the Morse code of telegraphy, which no one would suggest arose by chance. Just as with a telegraph message there is a structured sequence of dots and dashes, together with a universal code for translating the message, so with protein synthesis there is a structured sequence of nucleotides and a code to transcribe it. As well as matter (nucleotides and amino acids), there is information.

According to Shannon and Weaver's Information Theory, an input from an intelligent source is needed to produce information. A computer program requires an intelligent programmer. The information content of genetic material simply could not arise by the natural selection of random changes. So genetic information is conclusive proof that living things were indeed created.

Man a Single Species

Cells of all plants and animals (with the exception of bacteria and blue-green algae) contain various components outside of their nucleus. Of these, the mitochondria, which are involved in the production of energy from food using cytochrome-C, have small amounts of nucleic acid which in humans contains only 16,569 nucleotide pairs. This DNA, in humans, is inherited only from the mother. Comparisons of mitochondrial DNA in people of different races throughout the world have convinced some geneticists that all humans can trace their ancestry back to a single female – Eve, the mother of all living? The vast majority of mitochondrial DNA in all humans is identical, but mutations do occasionally occur. Estimates of the rate of mutation in mitochondrial DNA have caused scientists to date the first mother at some 200,000 years ago. Of course, this estimate is only as accurate as the estimate of mutation rate upon which it is based. And in any case this genetic evidence for the age of man is in marked contrast to the million or more years offered by palaeontologists who try to reconstruct man's evolution from questionable fossil fragments.

It is interesting to note that studies of genetic variation in nuclear genes of humans show that the variations between the genetic make-up of individuals from different ethnic groups is no greater than the variations found within a single group. The study of genetics does not support the idea that human races have evolved separately as Darwin thought, but that we all come from one set of parents.

In summary, we can say that as research reveals more and more of the ways in which characteristics are inherited from generation to generation, we find that the facts support special creation and oppose evolution theory. Mutations lead to a loss of information, and reshuffling of genes cannot produce novel information. Natural selection acts as a conserving agent, tending to eliminate mutants. Studies of genetic variation suggest that all people share a common ancestor who lived in the recent past. The chemical complexity of the manufacture of protein by DNA, (of which we have given but the barest outline), argues strongly for a Designer rather than a process based on chance. The information riding on the chemicals speaks unequivocally of an Intelligence.

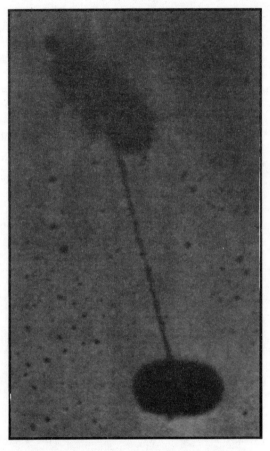

Two bacteria conjugating by means of a pilus are shown in the electron micrograph above.

Chapter 8

Is Evolution Possible?

There is a beauty and perfection apparent in all living things. Most forms of life exist in a number of variations, brought about either by natural selection or deliberate breeding. Creationists argue that there is a limit to the possible range of variations in a kind, which is governed by the genetic information in the wild type.

The idea that plants and animals gradually improve as they interact with their environment may seem plausible until one considers particular situations. We shall look at a few of these and conclude that because of the complexity of inter-meshing parts, evolution could not have produced them. They must perforce have been created fully formed and functioning.

Metamorphosis

A number of insects such as caddis flies and gnats, dragon-flies and moths, undergo one or two drastic changes during their life cycle in which the cells of an earlier stage decompose to form a culture medium for the growth of a new and different stage. A caterpillar changes into a chrysalis and then emerges as a butterfly.

The glow-worm, Arachnocampa luminosa, found in caves in New Zealand, emerges from the egg form as a larva.

71

During some nine months, the larva grows and moults four times, ultimately reaching a length of about an inch and a half. It spins a nest of silk from which it dangles a curtain of up to seventy threads studded with sticky droplets. These catch flying insects such as midges, and the larva pulls in the thread to devour its prey. The meals are attracted by the green glow in the tail of the larva. An enzyme, luciferase, acts upon the larva's excreta to produce the photochemical effect. After about nine months of feeding, the larva changes into a pupal stage which is only half as big, but continues to glow. In less than a fortnight, the winged imago emerges from the pupa. This fly stage is only half an inch long and has no mouth. It continues to emit luminescence, which now presumably helps in the finding of a mate. During from only one to three days, the female fly lays up to three hundred eggs before dying.

The larva is an eating machine; the fly an egg laying machine. Each stage is necessary for the continuance of the species. The information for larva, pupa and fly structures must all be present in the egg, together with the time switches to regulate the changes. Consider a prototype larva, the first to attempt to melt down into a pupa and then emerge as a fly. The enzymes which dissolve the body tissue of the larva must only go so far or the entire creature would disappear in a dying glow as luminous soup. And if it got that trick right first time, it still had to discover how to break out as an egg-laden fly. And presumably while it was trying to learn how to metamorphose, it was also busy evolving the knack of spinning a silk curtain to ensnare its first breakfast! Arachnocampa luminosa had to be created with all its varied genetic information complete at the beginning. The different stages could not have evolved independently.

Bombardier Beetle

Another little insect which could not evolve is the bombardier beetle, brachinus. This half inch long pyromaniac has chambers in its back end made of material which can withstand corrosive chemicals and explosions. It manufactures strong (25%) hydrogen peroxide, hydroquinones and an enzyme capable of catalysing the explosive reaction of these chemicals. When a predator approaches, the beetle shoots hot noxious gases from two adjustable nozzles at its rear end. The explosion, which can be heard as a sharp crack, consists of ejections of hot gases at the amazing rate of five hundred bursts a second. Again, consider the prototype bombardier beetle, still evolving its chemical defence mechanism. If the explosive components were not right, and properly timed, the beetle would fall prey to its predator. If it got its chemistry right, but had failed to evolve its nozzles, it would blow its own back end off. Here is another creature which could not evolve.

Fire Breathing Dinosaurs

Incidentally, some of the duck-billed dinosaur skeletons show structures in the dome of the skull which may well have been explosion chambers. These structures may have allowed the beasts to shoot out hot gases from their nostrils. Many cultures have folk memories of fire-breathing dragons. The biblical book of Job, in chapter 41, refers to Leviathan, a fierce creature with close set scales and terrible teeth. 'Out of his mouth go burning lights; sparks of fire shoot out. Smoke goes out of his nostrils, as from a boiling pot and burning rushes. His breath kindles coals, and a flame goes out of his mouth.' A partially evolved fire breathing dinosaur would rapidly become extinct!

Evolutionists say that dinosaurs became extinct 65 million years ago. However, on the 10th April, 1977 the remains of a plesiosaur was trawled up by Japanese fisherman from a depth of 900 feet off Christchurch, New Zealand. Those with a yen to see its picture should refer to Japanese postage stamps of the time.

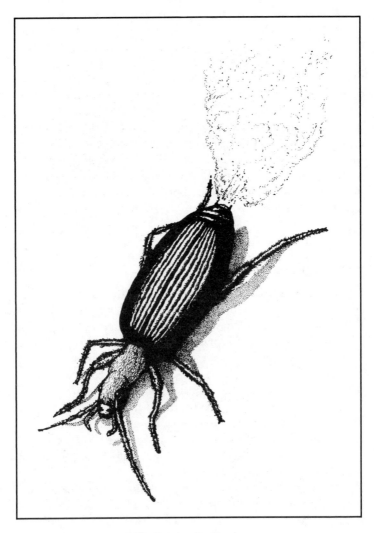

The Bombardier Beetle.

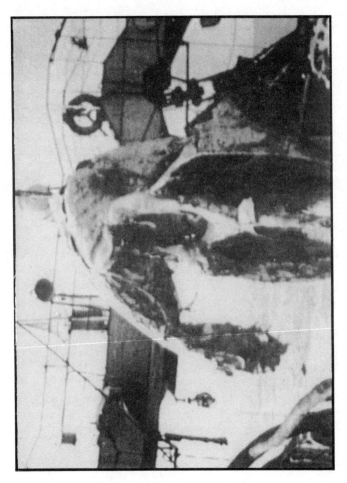

Japanese find plesiosaur? in 1977.

It had to be Right First Time

How did the sea slug gradually get the hang of eating sea anemones without digesting their poisonous exploding darts? How did it then learn to move these primed darts into the spurs on its own back ready to be shot at predators? How did migratory birds learn to follow the same paths as their ancestors without getting lost in the vastness of the oceans? How did bird's eggs survive while their parents were evolving the skills of nest-making? These are just a few examples of situations where everything had to be right from the beginning.

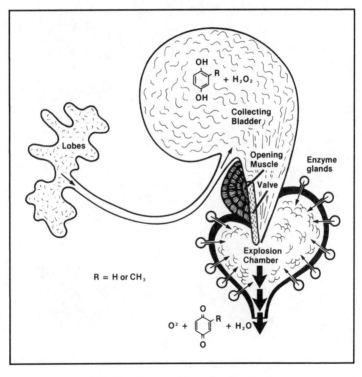

Explosion chamber of Bombardier Beetle.

Chapter 9

The Fossil Record

When one has concluded that there is no known mechanism for the process of evolution, one is still left with the fossil record which is generally interpreted as evidence for the grand ladder of life. However, not all experts think that fossils are evidence for evolution. Dr Mark Ridley, a palaeontologist at Oxford, wrote in the New Scientist in June 1981; 'No real evolutionist, whether gradualist or punctuationist, uses the fossil record as evidence in favour of the theory of evolution as opposed to Special Creation.'

No Intermediate Forms

Creatures appear in the fossil record fully formed. There are minor variations, just as one finds variation in living kinds. But the fossils show no emerging kind, no emerging organs such as the eye or a limb, and no intermediate forms. Darwin wrote; 'Why do we not find innumerable transitional forms embedded in countless numbers in the crust of the earth? Geology assuredly does not reveal any such finely graduated chain; and this, perhaps, is the most serious objection which can be urged against my theory.' Commenting on this in the nineteen fifties, Professor W.R. Thompson observed 'that the position is not notably different today. The modern

Darwinian palaeontologists are obliged, just like their predecessors and like Darwin, to water down the facts with subsidiary hypotheses which, however plausible, are in the nature of things unverifiable.' About the same time Professor Heribert-Nilsson wrote 'It is not even possible to make a caricature of an evolution out of palaeobiological facts ... the lack of transitional series cannot be explained as due to the scarcity of material.'

Writing in Creation, the journal of the Creation Science Movement, in May 1990, Mr John V. Collyer lists 16 quotations from encyclopedias, books and journals, all written by evolutionists and all bemoaning the missing links of geology. Unknown are the origins of star fish, horseshoe crabs, fishes, reptiles, their scales, the amniotic egg, limbs which are said to be derived from fins, seals, snakes, feathers which are said to be derived from scales, rabbits, New World monkeys, Old World monkeys and man. D.M. Raup, writing in the Field Museum of Natural History Bulletin for January 1979 says; 'Some of the classic cases of Darwinian change in the fossil record, such as the evolution of the horse, have had to be discarded.'

Fossil Kinds Unchanged

Not only are there no intermediate forms, but there is no sign of any change in the fossil beds beyond trivial variation. In the so-called Pre-Cambrian beds, fossil blue-green algae (stromatolites) are the same as blue-green algae found alive today. According to the geological time-scale these simple creatures have not evolved at all in two billion years. Horseshoe crabs dated at five hundred million years old are identical to horseshoe crabs alive today. Ferns dated at three hundred million years are just like their living counterparts, and quite unevolved. Insects embedded in amber, a fossilized tree resin, can be readily examined. Ants in amber are like their living cousins. Some have even been caught while milking aphids, just as they do today. And so we could go on

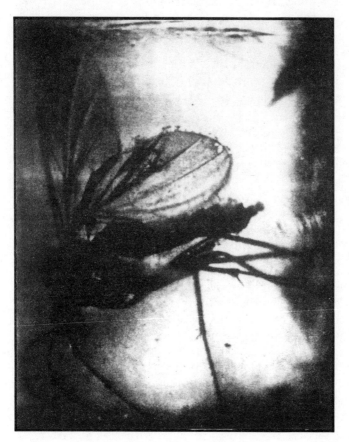

Insect in amber.

with a long list of creatures which have not changed at all over the time since they were petrified.

The coelacanth is a fish whose fins looked to the fertile imagination as though they were evolving into the flippers of an amphibian. It had last been seen in the sedimentary rocks which are reckoned to be seventy million years old. Here at last was a missing link! But then in 1938 a living coelacanth was fished up from the depths off Madagascar. It had not evolved into an amphibian! Why has it not turned up in the fossil record for seventy million years? Could it be that this time has only existed in the imaginations of geologists and astronomers? We shall need to return to this time scale. The coelacanth is by no means the only such creature to go missing only to turn up today. The tuatara reptile left no trace for an alleged 135 million years but today is alive and well and living in New Zealand.

Index Fossils

What can be deduced from the rocks about earth history? The bed-rock around the world is igneous in nature, being granite and basalt. It is composed of quartz and metal silicates as well as other minerals in a crystalline matrix. These rocks may be weathered by the action of waves, wind and frost to give broken materials, which if admixed with water may be deposited as sediment, becoming cemented together again as in sandstone. Some sedimentary rocks contain petrified plants and animals. These fossils are usually sorted into layers, often with just one type of creature at a given level, as for example the extensive shell fish beds. The rocks containing the simpler life-forms are said to be older than those with fossils of 'higher' animals, so that the chronological order of the rocks is explained according to an evolutionary interpretation. The fossil record is thus portrayed as a progression from simple to complex in older to younger rocks. R.H. Rastall, a Cambridge geologist wrote in the Encyclopaedia Britannica that 'It cannot be denied that from

LATIMERIA CHALUMNAE. J. L. B. Smith.
Museum, East London, South Africa.

Coelacanth.

a strictly philosophical standpoint geologists are here arguing in a circle. The succession of organisms has been determined by the remains embedded in the rocks, and the relative ages of the rocks are determined by the remains of the organisms that they contain.'

Rapid Burial

When a fish dies today, it is eaten by other sea creatures or it decomposes. To be fossilized it would need to be buried before it could rot or be eaten. So fossilization implies rapid burial, which in turn requires rapid rates of sedimentation. A large creature like a whale or dinosaur would be buried only under catastrophic conditions where tens of feet of sediment were being deposited in a short time. The same argument may be used over fossil upright trees, where the top must be covered before it has time to rot. There is evidence of some creatures being buried alive, which is certainly a rapid process! Fossil fish have been found in the act of swallowing smaller fry. Clams, which relax their muscles at death to open their shells, are found in the fossil state with closed valves. In many places whole beds are composed of fossils creating a massive fossil graveyard. This speaks of catastrophic conditions. Nor does fossilization necessarily require a long time period. Coal and oil have both been made in the laboratory using conditions of high pressure and temperature in as short a time as twenty minutes.

Rapid Rock Formation Demonstrated

In some parts of the world there have been vast magmatic intrusions covering hundreds of square miles with hot lava flows. This by its nature could not have been a slow process.

Where geologists come across rocks with fine layers they will interpret the strata as representing a year for each layer. Many rock formations are comprised of tens of thousands of such layers. In November, 1986, the French Academy of

Polystrate petrified tree.

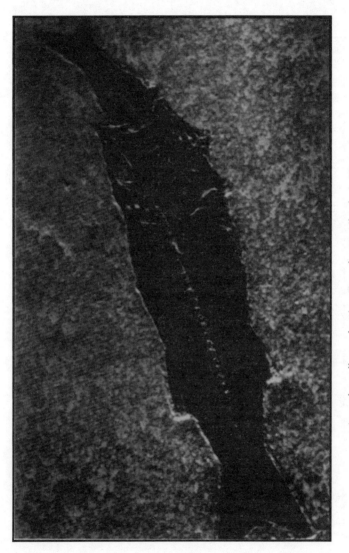

A perch swallows a herring. Found at Fossil Lake in Wyoming.

Science published some research of Guy Berthault. Berthault had taken a mixture of sands of two different grain sizes and poured the mix into both still and running water. As the sediment settled, it sorted itself into layers resembling laminated sedimentary rock. The thickness of the strata did not depend on the rate of deposition but on the difference in particle sizes of the mixture. This French scientist also took laminated rock and ground it up before pouring the particles into water. The original lamination was reproduced almost exactly. The layers do not take a year to form. They form as rapidly as the particles can settle.

World-wide Flood

The creationist looks for an explanation of a world-wide distribution of water-borne sediments containing rapidly formed fossils of all living types, and finds just such a scenario in the history book of Genesis. God said '*The end of all flesh is come before me; for the earth is filled with violence through them; and, behold, I will destroy them with the earth.*' A world-wide flood with accompanying volcanic activity ('*all the fountains of the great deep were broken up, and the windows of heaven were opened*') would have broken and churned up the rocks, destroying the earth. Massive tidal waves, circumnavigating the globe unhindered by land ('*and all the high hills, that were under the whole heaven, were covered.*') would erode the land beneath the surface. First to be buried in such a cataclysm would be the deep sea creatures. These would be followed by great shoals of fish and sharks, covered as they swam. Amphibians would be covered ahead of birds and mammals.

Evidence of such a world-wide flood is found in the folklore of all peoples. All such stories are slightly corrupted versions of the Scripture story, with God saving a family and representative creatures in a great boat. The Lord Jesus Christ, who created all things (John 1, Colossians 1, Hebrews 1), likens His second coming in judgement to the days of Noah and the Flood. He treats it as history (Matthew 24). Further, if the judgement of the Flood were not universal, by this comparison the final judgement would not be universal. The theistic evolutionist has here another theological problem.

Evidence from Catastrophe Today

Is the geological column the result of billions of years of slow weathering, or does it reflect the catastrophic effects of Noah's Flood and the Ice Age that followed it, with the division of the earth in the days of Peleg? Can big geological changes take place rapidly?

In 1980 in Washington State, USA, Mount St Helens erupted. An earthquake caused a massive rock-slide of half a cubic mile of rock from the top of the north face of the volcano. With the pressure suddenly released, superheated steam blasted out, flattening 150 square miles of forest in minutes. A further rock-slide sent a great wall of water over Spirit Lake, reaching 850 feet up the far slope and stripping the trees away. It is estimated that the total energy output was equal to 20,000 Hiroshima-size atom bombs. This local eruption would have been insignificant compared with the world-wide judgement in the days of Noah. However, 600 feet of stratified sediments accumulated rapidly. The strata did not represent annual or even seasonal deposits, as conventional geology would interpret such layers, but came all at once. Rills and gullies up to 125 feet deep have since been eroded in the still soft deposits of mud and pumice ash. Mud-flows carved a canyon system 140 feet deep in just one day. Millions of trees finished up in the waters of Spirit Lake, and tens of thousands of these have sunk to the bottom in an upright position, where they are being buried by continuing deposits of silt. Again, these deposits of upright trees would be interpreted as taking hundreds of years to form. Bark has been stripped from the floating log jam by the movement due to wind and waves. This has formed a layer of peat several inches thick.

Mount St. Helens.

Frozen Mammoths

The mammoths buried in the frozen tundra of Siberia and Canada are a second example of rapid geological change. Since the beginning of the twentieth century herds of frozen mammoths have been found in the permafrost. The story has gained credence that isolated mammoths fell into pits, got stuck in the mud, and became frozen. But there are thousands of them, all so well preserved that their meat is still edible. They are the world's most abundant source of ivory. These massive creatures were vegetarian, and each required an estimated 180 kg of plant food each day. A herd would require lush vegetation in stark contrast to the moss and stunted shrubs found in these latitudes today. Clearly the region had once had a very different climate. This was probably in recent times, since mammoths feature in cave paintings elsewhere.

The intriguing aspect of the demise of the mammoths is the suddenness with which it must have occurred. Fresh buttercups have been found in their mouths and in their stomachs. The colour of these flowers is destroyed rapidly by digestive juices at body temperature, so these huge carcasses must have frozen through to their middles before this decomposition could set in. Experts in the quick-freezing of food have judged that on a summer day in mid-summer (on the evidence of buttercups, etc.) the mammoths suffered a drop in temperature of a hundred degrees. The hitherto warm climate must then have become permafrost as it is today. If it had been permafrost before the animals died they could not have become immersed in it. If it had become defrosted at any time since this catastrophe, the meat would have rotted.

Recent Change in Earth's Axis?

It is not easy to explain a sudden and irreversible climate change of such a magnitude in the space of a few hours at most. A sudden shift in the earth's axis of rotation could

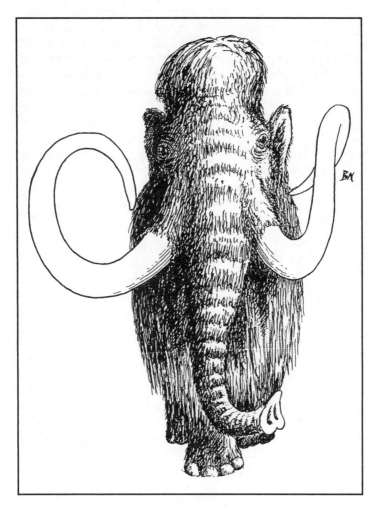

Mammoth.

change the latitude. The Australian astronomer G.F. Dodson has made a study of ancient upright pillars (gnomons) and sun temples. From sixty six records dating from ancient Egyptian and Chinese to Roman and Mediaeval times, he has plotted the history of recorded measurements of the angle of tilt of the earth's axis of rotation. It is clear from his plotted results that the earth is recovering from a major change in the angle of tilt of its axis. He estimates from the graph that this event took place around 2,350 BC. His revised angles of tilt bring the stone alignments at Stonehenge in southern England into agreement with the archaeologist's date of 350 BC for that megalithic circle. Further, the star positions as described by the Greek astronomer Eudoxus in 350 BC are confirmed by the revised angle of tilt as found by George Dodwell. (Dodwell was the South Australia Government Astronomer between 1909 and 1952.)

Interpreting the Geological Features

Here then, with Mt. St. Helens and with the frozen mammoths we have illustrations of how geological features can be formed within days or even hours. Such features would normally be explained by evolutionary geologists as the work of thousands of years. Once one has taken away the need for a time span of billions of years to interpret the geological features, evolution seems even less believable. We shall return to the subject of geological time in the next chapter. Meanwhile we have shown that the fossil record is most readily understood in terms of the created kinds being overtaken by a catastrophe. The supposed time span of billions of years is a smoke screen when interpreting geological features; and evolution as an explanation is even less believable.

Chapter 10

Dating the Past

Every schoolboy knows that the Normans invaded England in 1066. No one doubts that Julius Caesar had done the same in 55 BC (although we only have Caesar's own writings to go on!) Unless a record is kept at the time, dating even the recent past of our own family events can be uncertain. Back beyond the recorded testimony of history, indirect methods of dating must be used. Tree ring counts on the oldest living trees give an age of 4,568 years. This method of measuring time is thought to be correct within 10%. It has not proved possible to match patterns and go back before this time with dead trees. History and dendrochronology both go back to the world-wide flood.

The age given by popular science for the beginning of the universe is based upon a Big Bang scenario. With the demise of that theory, both the age and the size of the universe is open to question, since it can no longer be claimed that the red-shift of light is related to distance.

Age of Rocks

The age of the rocks, decreed by geologists such as Hutton and Lyell some 200 years ago, was based on the idea that sediments build up slowly over millions of years. Observations such as those at Mount St. Helens in Washington State,

USA, which erupted in 1980, have shown that rapid cata-strophic events are a more likely mechanism. If the majority of the geological column is attributable to the world-wide flood recorded by history, the geological time scale disap-pears.

In the twentieth century, the dates allotted to rocks by Hutton have seemingly been confirmed by radiometric dat-ing. The layman does not realize, however, that these methods give widely discordant results. Ages which agree with the expected geological date are accepted, while those which are at variance with the assumed time are discarded and remain unpublished. Richard Leakey's '1470 Man' was variously dated using the same rocks, the same equipment and the same technicians, at both 220 million years and 2.6 million years BP. Similarly, rocks associated with Louis Leakey's 'Nutcracker Man' gave a date of 1.75 million years, although material from the same stratum submitted to car-bon 14 dating gave an age of 10,000 years. A single sample of rock, one of many brought back from the moon, was dated by the uranium-thorium-lead method to give results ranging from 5.4 billion years (somewhat more than the estimated age of the moon) to 28.1 billion years (half as old again as the greatest estimate of the age of the universe!) Results have been published that show that recently erupted rocks have been dated at 22 million years old by the K:Ar method, and living snails were found to be 27,000 years old by the Car-bon 14 method! The hair on a mammoth was found to be 26,000 years old while the peat in which the mammoth was preserved was measured by the same C 14 technique and found to be only 5,600 years old.

Assumptions of Radiometric Dating

The dating laboratory is not measuring a date directly. It is measuring the relative amounts of two radio isotopes. Since one may be formed from the other, and the present rate of this transmutation can be estimated, the results may be used to derive an age. One has to assume that all of the daughter element was formed as a result of decay of the parent element and that no daughter element was originally present in the rock. This assumption cannot, of course be verified. One has also to assume that the rate of decay has been constant over vast periods of time and has not been affected by a flux of high energy particles at any time in the earth's past. Recent research on the variation in the velocity of light makes it possible that decay rates have also been much greater in the past, since they are dependent on the speed of light. One has further to assume that no parent or daughter element has migrated into or out of the sample during its history. Since many of the radiometric processes involve gases and water soluble elements, this assumption is also unwarranted.

This is rather like coming into a bathroom and finding a tap running and a partially filled bath. One can estimate the time since the tap was turned on from the volume of water in the tub and the rate of flow from the tap. One's estimate assumes that the bath was empty when the tap was turned on, that the water pressure has not varied to affect the flow rate, and that the plug is not leaking. A catastrophic event such as someone tipping several buckets of water into the bath would render one's estimate meaningless.

Indications of a Young Age

It is not generally publicized that there are a number of measurements which give a young age for the earth and the universe.

Oceans

If we measure the rates at which salts are being added to the oceans by river and coastal erosion, we arrive at an age for the oceans which varies for different salts from a few thousand years to a few hundred million years, but not the billions of years required by the evolutionists. Of course, if the oceans were created already salted, and if most of the erosion was catastrophic, we must revise even these comparatively young ages downward.

Earth's Magnetic Field

The earth's magnetic field was first measured by Gauss in 1835. In subsequent measurements it has been found that the magnetic field strength is diminishing exponentially with time. The time required for the magnetic field strength to fall to half of its present value is calculated to be only 1,400 years. This means that in 600 AD the earth's magnetism was twice as strong as at present, while in 800 BC it was four times its present strength, and in 2,200 BC it had a value eight times the present value. Extrapolating back in time, we find that only 10,000 years ago the earth would have had the magnetic strength of a magnetic star. Life could not be supported on such a hot planet. From these observations, we deduce that the earth cannot be as much as 10,000 years old. The evolutionists have to postulate that there have been several magnetic reversals in the past, and cite the direction of the field in minerals in the rocks. However, if these magmatic rocks were the result of vulcanism during the flood (the fountains of the great deep were broken up) when the earth's axis may well have been oscillating, varying field directions might be expected.

Meteoric Dust

Artificial satellites have been used to measure the rate at which meteoric dust settles to earth. It was estimated that some 14.3 million tons of dust settled to earth each year. This, in the thousands of millions of years of alleged earth history, would have given a layer some 54 feet thick all over the surface of the earth. Wind, erosion and sea floor spreading might be expected to sweep away some of the dust. Yet there is not that much nickel, a major constituent of this deposit, in the earth's crust. The moon has no atmosphere or oceans to disperse the dust, and the Apollo team were concerned that thick dust would be a hazard in landing a craft on the moon. In the event, the dust turned out to be only about an eighth of an inch in thickness corresponding to less than ten thousand years.

That there is any cosmic dust at all in the solar system is evidence that it is not billions of years old. The pressure of solar radiation slowly sweeps up the interplanetary dust into the sun. This is known as the Poynting-Robertson effect. By this action, the dust should have been swept clear within only two and a half million years (not tens of billions of years).

The New Moon

The moon probes have also revealed that the moon is still cooling down. This is contrary to expectation for a body of that size with an estimated age of 4.5 billion years. The moon has a large temperature radiance at the surface. The presence of a magnetic field indicates that it has a fluid core. Instruments left on the moon have registered moonquakes.

The moon is receding from the earth by about two inches a year as the earth gives up angular momentum to its satellite. Two billion years ago, less than half the accepted age of the earth-moon system, the moon would have been so close to the earth that tidal forces would have torn it apart. Also the earth would have been spinning on its axis very rapidly, resulting in violent climatic conditions.

Short Term Comets

Comets circulate around our sun in elliptical orbits. On their journey near the sun material is lost from these 'dirty snowballs' in a visible tail. Short term comets such as Halley's Comet would evaporate completely in less than a million

The Moon – a young planet.

years. There is no satisfactory explanation for the existence of short period comets except that the solar system is less than a million years old. There is no positive evidence for a cloud of comets beyond visible detection, as proposed by Oort.

Globular clusters of stars within our own galaxy, the Milky Way, are moving so fast that they would escape from the galaxy within a million years. Their presence, moving at such speeds, denies a multi-billion year old universe.

Possible Decrease in the Velocity of Light

A problem for those who believe that the creation took place only some 6,000 years ago is that light appears to have taken millions of years to reach us from distant galaxies. The supernoval explosion witnessed in 1987 seems to be an event which occurred before God stretched out the heavens! Great distances in the universe are measured, not by trigonometry (a bit like trying to measure the difference in angles of a chimney stack 20 miles away as seen by your right eye and then your left eye), but by the assumption that red-shift is proportional to distance. This is based on the discredited Big Bang Theory. As we have already discussed in chapter 3, a Russian scientist, V. Troitskii, of the Radiophysical Research Institute, Gorky, has suggested (Astrophysics and Space Science, vol 139, (1987) 389–411) that the red-shift is due, not to a receding star or galaxy, but to a decrease in the velocity of light. In 1984, an American scientist, T. van Flandern, of the US National Bureau of Standards, published his findings (NBS (US) Special Publication 617 (1984)) saying that the atomic clock was slowing down relative to astronomical time. From 1955 to 1981, time as measured by the caesium clock was slowing down relative to time as measured by the orbit of the moon around the earth. The vibrations of the atom are linked to the speed of light, so here was an indication that light is slowing down.

The speed of light has been measured many times by 16

different methods over the past 300 years. Some methods are more accurate than others and give a smaller spread of experimental error. Australian scientists B. Setterfield and T. Norman have analysed published measurements of the speed of light (SRI Internat. Technical Report, August 1987). Their plot of measured speed of light against date of measurement shows a curve indicating a significant decrease in the measured velocity of light from the earliest measurements to the present time. Setterfield did not discover this effect himself, for it had been commented upon in the science journals over the years. Now he has plotted out the results and discussed the implications for a young universe. Extending his graph backwards in time gives a speed of light approaching infinity some 6,000 years ago.

Superluminaries

Not only does a decrease in the velocity of light with time allow light to reach the earth from distant galaxies within historical time, but it supplies an explanation for an effect that has long puzzled astronomers. In many distant galaxies, objects have been observed moving relative to each other at speeds many times the present speed of light. Relativity theory forbids this. However, if we are seeing them in the past when the value of the speed of light was orders of magnitude greater, then they are not exceeding the speed limit.

Rates of Radioactive Decay

It can be shown that many physical quantities are directly or inversely proportional to the speed of light. Planck's seemingly misnamed Constant is inversely proportional to the speed of light. (Planck's Constant is the ratio of the energy to the frequency of light. This energy, of course, remains constant, while frequency is the ratio of the speed of light to its wave-length. If the speed of light were greater in the past, as seen in distant galaxies, then the wave-length must have been longer to maintain constant energy. Hence the red-shift is explicable in terms of a decreasing speed of light.) Measurements of Planck's 'Constant' over the past century show that it is increasing in value, as predicted for a decrease in the speed of light. More to the point while considering the evidence for a young earth, radioactive decay rates are directly proportional to the speed of light. This means that if light is slowing down, then decay rates were much faster in the past, and consequently times for decay were much shorter. Ages of hundreds of millions of years are reduced to only thousands of years, in line with a biblical time-scale.

An Impossibly Young Creation?

It will be seen from the foregoing that the only reason for not accepting a 6,000 year old universe is the need to accommodate evolution. Before the end of the eighteenth century, most scientists were comfortable with a biblical time-frame from Creation to the Second Coming. The evolutionary time-scale ignores many effects which demand a comparatively young universe.

In a report in the journal 'Geotimes' in September, 1978, the Astrophysicist Dr John Eddy wrote; 'I suspect that the Sun is 4.5 billion years old. However, given some new and unexpected results to the contrary, and some time for frantic readjustment, I suspect that we could live with Bishop Ussher's value for the age of the Earth and Sun (approx 6,000 yrs). I don't think we have much in the way of observational evidence in astronomy to conflict with that.'

Since that was said in 1978, 'new and unexpected results' have included the anisotropy of the universe compared with the smoothness of the background radiation, leading to the abandonment of the Big Bang theory of cosmogony. The evidence for the decrease in the speed of light is far from being generally accepted, but this is probably because of the implications for a young universe. The laboratory evidence of rapid sedimentation rates by Guy Berthault and the field evidence from the Mt. St. Helens eruption have also come since Dr Eddy's remarks were printed. We submit that the time for 'frantic readjustment' has come.

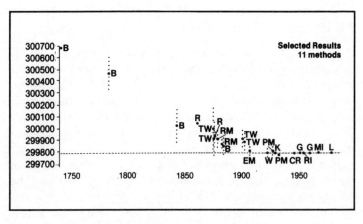

Decrease in the measured speed of light.

Chapter 11
Supposed Human Evolution

Evolutionists are not very impressed by the Genesis account of how mankind arrived on the earth. They have produced a modest number of fossils which they claim show a progression from ape to man. (All of the fossil fragments used as evidence for ape-men would fit easily into a single coffin – and this would be the best place for them!)

This claim of human evolution has been bolstered by two erroneous ideas; that the human embryo recapitulates its evolutionary history during development in the womb, and that the human body contains many vestigial parts, now useless, which had been vital in our evolutionary past. Before discussing the ape-man fossils, we will look briefly at recapitulation theory and vestiges.

Recapitulation Theory

The recapitulation theory was thought by Darwin to be the most important evidence for evolution. It was developed by Ernst Haeckel, a contemporary of Darwin, and has been summed up by the phrase 'Ontogeny recapitulates phylogeny.' This impressive scientific jargon may be translated; The development of the embryo passes through the evolutionary history of the animal.

The human embryo starts life as a single cell in a watery

environment, just as life is said to have begun. And just as life is said to have evolved through fishes, the human embryo at an early stage appears to have gill slits. Later it appears to have a tail like a monkey, before being born as a fully human baby.

The fertilized egg, however, does not function as a single celled protozoon. At this stage it has all the genetic information for the development of the egg into a collection of differentiated cells and on to the baby and through to the adult. It rapidly divides and subdivides. Furthermore, the so-called gill slits are ridges which grow into parts of the tongue, lower jaw and neck. They do not have a breathing function, and it is dishonest for evolutionists to continue, as they do, to call them gill slits. The tail, also, is an illusion, being the backbone, with only 33 vertebrae at all stages of development. Due to different rates of growth of the parts of the foetus, it does stick out a bit. In the same way, the head of the foetus is disproportionately large, but no one would claim that we came from large headed ancestors.

Haeckel's diagrams were particularly convincing, and he later admitted that they were intentionally changed and exaggerated to fit the theory. He was convicted of this fraud by a university court at Jena. Sir Gavin de Beer of the British Museum has said, 'Seldom has an assertion like that of Haeckel's theory of recapitulation, facile, tidy and plausible, widely accepted without critical examination, done so much harm to science.'

Vestiges

The evolution model claims that as a species undergoes mutation to become something different, and adapts to a changing environment, any anatomical parts no longer needed by the changed organism become redundant. The whale has bones thought to be vestiges of hind legs, but these bones serve as essential anchors for muscles. The tail of the monkey is said to become the coccyx in the human. In fact, muscles are also anchored to the coccyx, and these facilitate the excretion of waste products. The coccyx performs a vital function. Only to the zealous evolutionist could it appear to be a vestige of our imagined monkey ancestry.

A generation ago it was claimed that there were 180 vestigial organs in man, but as knowledge of their function has increased, their number has dropped to about half a dozen. For example, the pituitary gland was once considered vestigial, but is now called the master gland. The thyroid, ear muscles and appendix are all now known to have uses. The thymus is a small shrivelled gland in man compared to some animals, but its function has recently been found. With the advent of transplant surgery, it was discovered that the thymus is the body's centre for combating foreign bodies. It was also found that the tonsils and appendix are rich in antibodies, being also part of the immune system.

Professor Goodrich of Oxford has said 'He would be a rash man indeed who would now assert that any part of the body is useless.'

Of course, if all kinds of creatures were created, we would not expect to find vestigial parts. Rather we would expect special designs to meet particular needs, such as the thumb of the panda which equips it so well to strip the bark from its bamboo food.

The evolutionist, however, goes through all sorts of contortions to explain the way things are, as witness the following example taken from the Encyclopaedia Britannica (15th Edition, 1974) article on Morphology:

> 'The present-day Australian tree-climbing kangaroos, for example, are the descendants of a ground-dwelling marsupial, from whom evolved forms that began to live in trees and eventually developed limbs adapted to tree climbing. But the events may have occurred in the reverse sequence: that is, specialized limbs may have evolved before the animal adopted an arboreal mode of life. In any event, some of the tree kangaroos subsequently left the trees, became readapted to life on the

ground (i.e. their hindlegs became adapted for leaping), and then went back to the trees but with legs so highly specialized for leaping as to be useless in grasping a tree trunk: consequently, present-day tree kangaroos climb by bracing their feet against a tree trunk, as do bears.'

Because the hind legs are designed for leaping, the fused second and third toes are described as vestigial! This sort of explanation is reminiscent of the story of how the elephant got its trunk, by having its nose repeatedly pulled by a crocodile when it went to the water-hole!

Chapter 12

Monkey Business

Java Man – Pithecanthropus Erectus

Following the writings of Darwin and Huxley, it was expected that fossil ape-men would be found. In the closing decade of the nineteenth century, a Dutch surgeon, Eugene Dubois, went to Java specifically to search for missing ancestors. He found a seam of rock rich in fossil bones. He selected a fossil skull-cap of a giant gibbon, some molar teeth, a fragment of lower jaw and a human thigh bone. He also found some human skulls and other human bones, but he kept quiet about these. It would not do to find man and his ancestors in the same fossil beds.

Dubois exhibited his gibbon skull-cap and human femur all over Europe, claiming that they belonged to a single individual. In fact the bones had been found 45 feet apart, the femur a year after the discovery of the skull portion. Because the femur suggested a bipedal gait while the skull-cap was ape like, the finds were labelled Pithecanthropus Erectus – Upright Ape-man.

Dubois' mentor, Ernst Haeckel of Recapitulation Theory fame, wrote that Pithecanthropus Erectus 'was truly a Pliocene remainder of that famous group of the higher Catarrhines, which were the immediate pithecoid ancestors of man. He is indeed the long-searched-for Missing Link.'

Sir Grafton Elliot Smith, FRS, Professor of Anatomy at Manchester, declared, 'The amazing thing had happened. Dubois had actually found the fossil his scientific imagination had visualized.' Another expert, Dr Frederick Tilney, examined the skull-cap and suggested from the markings that the ape-man could talk!

Although Dubois only had a skull-cap, his scientific imagination enabled him to estimate the brain capacity of Java Man to be 900 cm^3, intermediate between those of apes and men. He constructed a model of the complete ape-man. G.K. Chesterton was moved to write '...people talked of Pithecanthropus as of Pitt or Fox or Napoleon. Popular histories published portraits of him like the portraits of Charles I or George IV. A detailed drawing was produced, carefully shaded to show the very hairs of his head were all numbered. No uninformed person, looking at its carefully limned face, would imagine for a moment that this was the portrait of a thigh bone, of a few teeth and a fragment of a cranium.'

Some scientists of the day were also critical of Dubois' finds. Professor Virchow said 'In my opinion this creature was an animal, a giant gibbon in fact. The thigh bone has not the slightest connection with the skull.'

In the late 1930s, von Koenigswald found part of a skull in Java. He offered local tribesmen ten cents for every piece they found like it. He was handed forty fragments, freshly broken up to earn more bounty! The skull reconstructed from the pieces was used to support the contention that Pithecanthropus Erectus was an ancestor of man.

Piltdown Man – Eoanthropus

In 1908, in a gravel bed at Piltdown Farm, near Lewes in Sussex, England, workmen smashed into what they described as a bone coconut. A local solicitor, Charles Dawson, who was an amateur archaeologist, recognized it as a fossil skull. Dawson, too, was looking for the transitional

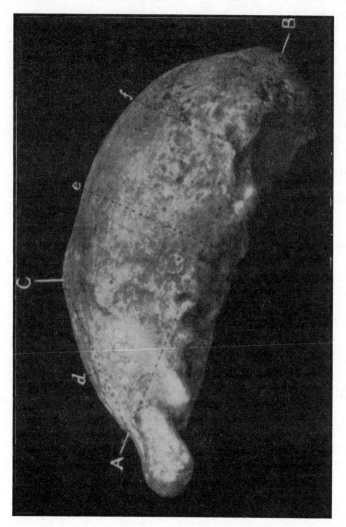

Cranial Dome of *Pithecanthropus erectus* from river gravel in Java.

ape-man. He had already been fortunate enough to spot a sea-serpent off Hastings Pier. This combination of expectancy and gullibility qualified him admirably to be the discoverer of Eoanthropus dawsonii – Dawson's Dawn Man – the most celebrated hoax in the history of science.

Dawson was joined in the excavations at Piltdown by, among others, Sir Arthur Smith-Woodward, FRS, Keeper of the Geological Department of the British Museum. Also helping was Pierre Teilhard de Chardin, a Jesuit priest who was subsequently to find missing links in Pekin and elsewhere, and write many volumes linking evolution and Christianity. Between them they uncovered other bones, some teeth and a part of a lower jaw. Unfortunately, the jaw was broken at the point where it should have articulated with the cranium. The jaw was ape-like, the cranium like a man; truly a transitional form.

In his book, *The Antiquity of Man*, Sir Arthur Keith, FRS, wrote 'That we should discover such a race as Piltdown, sooner or later, has been an article of faith in the anthropologist's creed ever since Darwin's time.' In 1938 Keith had the honour of unveiling a memorial to his ancestor at the Piltdown site. No self-respecting museum was without its reconstruction of the skull, the head or even the whole shambling, hairy ape-man. Smith-Woodward wrote a first hand account of the discovery in a book called *The First Englishman*. Public houses in the vicinity were named after Piltdown Man, the tavern signs an eloquent education to the wayfarer. At a less serious level, several hundred doctoral theses addressed the subject at universities around the world.

Piltdown Man fooled the experts for forty years, being eventually debunked in 1951, when the jaw and cranium were found to have differing proportions of fluoride. A careful reappraisal revealed that while the original 'coconut' was the cranium of a man a few thousand years old, the jaw was that of a modern orang-utan. The jaw had been coloured with the chemical potassium dichromate to give the appearance of age and the teeth had been filed down to resemble those of a man.

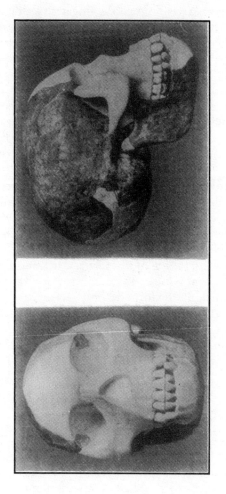

Piltdown Man.

Initially, the blame for the fraud was laid on the late Charles Dawson, the only amateur involved. Others have sought to implicate the British Museum, and a recent American writer (1990) has pointed the finger at Keith. A letter to the New Scientist (4 Jan, 1971) made it clear that some of the local people at Piltdown suspected Teilhard de Chardin. Many of the fraudulent items had been found by Teilhard, though they may have been planted by another. One such item was a canine tooth, which had been filed down, packed with sand grains and stained with dichromate. Those present congratulated him on spotting something so inconspicuous in the gravel. Another such tooth found by this philosopher has since been found to be radio-active, a property of which the hoaxer would not have been aware in 1912. Its radio-activity profile has revealed its origin as Ichkeul in Tunisia, a site not publicly identified until 1918. Teilhard de Chardin had been a lecturer in Chemistry at Cairo from 1906 to 1908, and his interest in fossils makes it probable that he had visited this North African site.

In his book *Unveiling Man's Origin* Dr Louis Leakey says 'There can be no doubt that at least one of the people involved in making the forgeries must have had considerable knowledge of chemistry as well as some training in geology and human anatomy. The perpetrators also must have had access to fossil bones from outside Great Britain.' This description is virtually a photo-fit picture of Teilhard de Chardin.

Nebraska Man – Hesperopithecus

In 1921, Professor Henry Fairfield Osborne from Nebraska, USA, visited London and was impressed by the Piltdown fossils. When, the following year, a fossilized tooth was unearthed in Nebraska, he had no reservations in hailing it as that of another missing link. Sir Grafton Elliot Smith in his *Evolution of Man* (1924) enthused, 'To the two extinct genera Pithecanthropus and Eoanthropus, it is now proposed to

Sir Arthur Keith unveils the Memorial to the Piltdown 'Man', July 22, 1938. The inscription runs: *Here in the old river gravel Mr. Charles Dawson, F.S.A., found the fossil skull of Piltdown Man, 1912–13.*

add a third, Hesperopithecus, the Ape Man of the Western World.' The Illustrated London News showed a picture of Mr and Mrs Hesperopithecus, complete with assorted prehistoric creatures, in a two page spread.

All this was very gratifying for Osborne, especially so since a local politician, W.J. Bryan, was campaigning to outlaw the teaching of evolution in schools. The Hesperopithecus tooth was cited as evidence in the famous Scopes trial, where a schoolteacher was found guilty of teaching evolution theory as fact. (The film, *Inherit the Wind* dramatizes the Scopes trial, guiding the cinema-goer's sympathies towards the progressive, scientific teacher, and against the religious bigotry of the prosecution.) Osborne declared 'The Earth spoke to Bryan from his own state of Nebraska. The Hesperopithecus tooth is like a still, small voice. Its sound is by no means easy to hear... This little tooth speaks volumes of truth, in that it affords evidence of man's descent from the ape.'

A few years later more teeth were found, attached to a jawbone. It transpired that Nebraska Man had in fact been neither ape nor man, but a kind of pig. This volume of truth was not publicized!

Pekin Man – Sinanthropus Pekinensis

The missing link fever continued unabated through the 1920s and 1930s, with Dr Davidson Black and Father Teilhard de Chardin both moving from Piltdown to Pekin, China. In a cave they discovered the broken skulls of twenty four creatures in a layer of compressed ash some twenty two feet thick. The reconstructed skulls were all broken at the base, as if to extract the edible brains. Most were incomplete. In spite of the difficulty in reconstructing fragmented skulls, a brain capacity of over 1,000 cm^3 was assigned, placing Sinanthropus between apes and men. A reconstruction was given female features and called Nellie.

The archaeologist M. Boule studied the bones at the cave

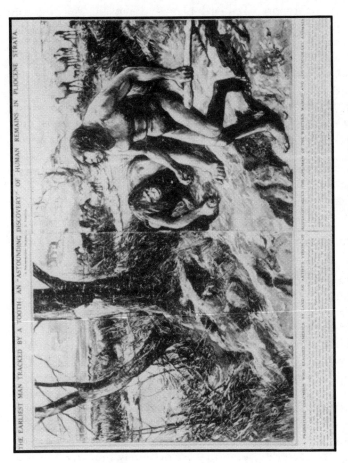

THE EARLIEST MAN TRACKED BY A TOOTH AN ASTOUNDING DISCOVERY OF HUMAN REMAINS IN PLIOCENE STRATA

Hesperopithecus – reconstructed from a pig's tooth.

and concluded that they were skulls of apes, killed by real men for their edible brains. He reported, 'Sinanthropus appears in its deposit only in the guise of a mere hunter's prey.'

In his report, Teilhard played down the massive ash deposits, referring to them as 'traces of ash'! Clearly real men were here, probably burning lime for building. Bolas stones were found, which require considerable skill to make and wield. In 1929 the press reported the discovery by the chief Chinese archaeologist at the site, Pei, of ten skeletons of men, including a perfect skull, in the cave. Since then, however, nothing more has been heard of these finds, and the broken monkey skulls are still hailed as missing links. The evidence was unaccountably lost when China was overrun during World War II. Teilhard de Chardin, who remained in Pekin throughout the Japanese occupation, makes no mention of their disappearance in his writings.

Decline in Integrity

Professor W.R. Thompson, in his Introduction to the Everyman 1956 edition of Darwin's *Origin of Species*, wrote; 'The success of Darwinism was accompanied by a decline in scientific integrity. This is already evident in the reckless statement of Haeckel and in the shifting, devious, and histrionic argumentation of T.H. Huxley. A striking example, which has only recently come to light, is the alteration of the Piltdown skull so that it could be used as evidence for the descent of man from the apes; but even before this a similar instance of tinkering with evidence was finally revealed by the discoverer of Pithecanthropus [Dubois], who admitted, many years after his sensational report, that he had found in the same deposits bones that are definitely human.'

Thompson went on to describe the idea promulgated by evolutionists, that categories of living things are not fixed and that limits to variation do not exist, as 'unverifiable speculation'. He continued; 'Thus are engendered those fragile towers of hypotheses based on hypotheses, where fact and fiction intermingle in an inextricable confusion.'

Anti-God Philosophy

In the same Introduction to the 'Origin', Professor Thompson wrote: 'The doctrine of evolution by natural selection as Darwin formulated, and as his followers still explain it, has a strong anti-religious flavour.' As we have seen, some of the scientists involved in the ape-man controversy risked their reputations by deliberate fraud. For most, however, their mistakes are probably attributable to a mixture of ambition and self-deception. Their self-deception was fired in many cases by a desire to dethrone the Creator in the minds of men.

This is illustrated in the final section of the article on 'Evolution' in the 15th Edition of the Encyclopaedia Britannica (1974) written by Sir Gavin de Beer of the British Museum. He writes: 'Darwin did two things: he showed that evolution was a fact contradicting scriptural legends of creation and that its cause, natural selection, was automatic with no room for divine guidance or design. Furthermore, if there had been design, it must have been very maleficent to cause all the suffering and pain that befall animals and men. In 1860 T.H. Huxley demolished the arguments of Bishop Samuel Wilberforce. In the famous 'monkey trial' conviction of schoolteacher John T. Scopes in 1925, a Tennessee law banning the teaching of evolution was upheld, but years later, in 1968, the United States Supreme Court ruled that anti-evolution laws were unconstitutional.'

This anti-God teaching in our schools, in the name of science, has now influenced generations of our children. Is it coincidental that church attendance has diminished, moral standards have become eroded, crime rates have soared, divorce is now regarded as the norm, abortion is not only legal but commonplace and sexual deviation has become widely acceptable? The Christian teaching on the God-appointed family pattern and the sanctity of human life are derived directly from the account of the Creation in Genesis. By attacking this foundation, evolutionary teaching has caused the collapse of the moral edifice which is the basis of society. Evolution is not a take-it-or-leave-it side issue.

Tell a child that he has not been made in the image of God, but that he has an animal ancestry, and all the rest follows as predictably as night follows day.

Chapter 13

More Ancestors

Apart from the skulduggery referred to in the previous section, other candidates for man's ancestral line are all either apes or men.

Fossil Apes

Although experts in this field have not reached a consensus and new fossil finds can play havoc with cherished theories, many believe that the fossil ape Ramapithecus was an early forerunner of man. Dated at two million years BP (before present – evolutionists show a reluctance to use the BC and AD of real history), this species is known from just a couple of dozen jaws and some teeth found in India. Its status as our ancestor is founded upon the shape of the jaw. The teeth in the jaw have certain characteristics which are also found in man. However, the Gelada baboon, alive and well and living in Ethiopia today, has similar teeth, but has no human characteristics.

Also in our line of descent, according to many anthropologists, are the Australopithecines or southern apes. Some nearly complete skulls found by Richard Leakey in East Africa have brain capacities of apes. A complete skeleton of a man was found in the same vicinity as long ago as 1913 by Professor Hans Reck.

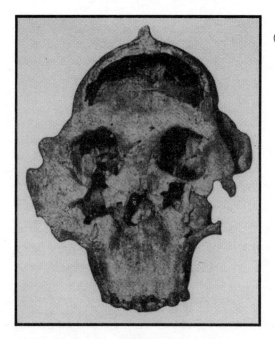

(a) Skull

(b) Drawn for *The Sunday Times* 5th April, 1964. By kind permission of *The Sunday Times*.

Zinjanthropus: (b), (c) and *(d)* are artists impressions of 'ape-man'.

(c) Drawn by Neave Parker for Dr L.S.B. Leakey. Copyright, *The Illustrated London News & Sketch, Ltd.*, 9th January, 1960.

(d) Drawn by Maurice Wilson for Dr Kenneth P. Oakley. By kind permission of Dr Kenneth P. Oakley.

The dates given for these fossils can be very confusing. They are arrived at by the potassium-argon method (see chapter 10). Scientists are not here measuring a number of years as you might suppose. They are measuring the relative amounts of isotopes of two elements, potassium (K) and argon (Ar), in rocks associated with the fossils. Then using a mathematical formula which involves several assumptions, an age is calculated. Small variations in the K:Ar ratio cause widely ranging results. For example, 'Lucy', an ape found by D. Johanson in Ethiopia in the 1970s was variously dated at 3.1 to 5.3 million years. In the same decade, R. Leakey found a 'hominid' catalogued as '1470 Man' which was variously dated by the British Museum as 220 million and 2.6 million years old! Argon is a gas which can migrate within a mineral, while potassium salts are soluble in water. It is hardly surprising that the method is unreliable.

Neanderthal Man

Homo Neanderthalensis fossils are widespread. These men were short, heavily built, with enlarged joints, and ridges across their brows. Their brain capacity was about 2,000 cm^3, larger than most people alive today. The famous nineteenth century anatomist R. Virchow claimed that Neanderthal Man was a true man who suffered from rickets and arthritis. However, following Darwin, opinion shifted and he became an ape-like ancestor of man. In the last 25 years, opinion has swung back, and scientists claim that his teeth and bones show evidence of a lack of vitamin D, even in young children. Perhaps dietary deficiencies, possibly lack of sunshine in northern Europe during the Ice Age that followed Noah's Flood, produced arthritis and rickets, as manifested in the enlarged joints. As to the facial characteristics, they are not unknown in people today, and eyebrow ridges are noticeable on prehistoric carvings and paintings.

Neanderthals buried their dead, painted pictures and fashioned elegant tools. Yet an illustration in *New Scientist* in 1991 showed him as an ape!

HOMO NEANDERTHALENSIS
(*possibly Homo sapiens*)

MONTE CIRCEO

Discoverer :   BLANC*, 1939.

Location :   Monte Circeo, cave. Pontine Plain, South of Rome.

Age in years : B.P. 35,000—70,000. A_3 dating.

See :   Sergi, S., 'Il cranio neandertaliano del Monte Circéo.'

    (*Rendiconti della R. Acc dei Lincei* XXIX, 6a, Rome, 1939).

    Blanc, A. C., 'L'Homme fossile du Monte Circéo.' (*L'Anthropologie*, XLIX, 1939).

*—Professor (Baron) A. C. Blanc of Rome University.

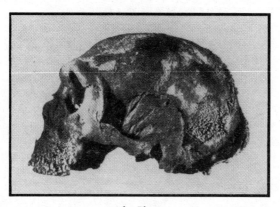

(after Blanc).

Neanderthal skull.

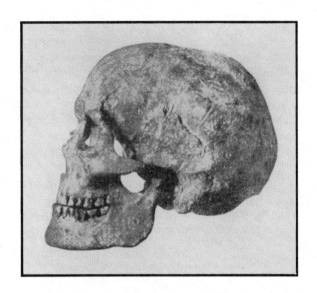

CRO-MAGNON (Europe)
(*Homo sapiens*)

Found in :   1868.

Discoverer :   Louis Lartet.

Location :   Cro-Magnon, Dordogne. France.

Age :   20,000–30,000 B.P. A_4 dating.

Description :   Skull of man aged about 50 years.
Cephalic index : 73.7 approx.
Capacity : 1590 cc. approx.
Heads of this type are still surviving in the Dordogne and parts of Sweden.
See : de Quatrefages and Hamy. *Crania Ethnica*, (1882) p. 91.

See : Vallois, H., La durée de la vie chez l'Homme fossile. *L'Anthropologie*, XLVII, 1937, p. 499.
Keane, A. H., *Ethnology* (1896).

Cro-Magnon skull.

Tertiary Man

Along with Neanderthals, other races of men left their remains world-wide. Cro-Magnon Man was a healthy six-footer who would be easily lost in a crowd on Waterloo Station, provided he had a shirt and jeans. Evolutionists have no problem with such fossil men, since they are found in the uppermost (Quaternary) sediments. However, pertinent to our discussion are the discoveries of remains and artifacts of true men at levels below the Quaternary. These would appear to make man contemporary with, or even older than his ancestors. Evolutionists overcome this problem by insisting that these are intrusive burials, or practical jokes, or by simply ignoring them altogether. These early remains include the Castenedolo Skull, the Calaveras Skull, the Foxhall Jaw, the Galley Hill Skeleton and many others. For a detailed consideration of these the reader is referred to *Fossil Man* by Frank Cousins (Creation Science Movement, 1971) and to *Ape-Men – Fact or Fallacy* by Malcolm Bowden (Sovereign Publications, 1977). Many of these remains were found by specialists who attested to the fact that the overlying strata had not been disturbed by burial.

Archaeological Remains

If Man has been around for a million years, why is it that the oldest buildings and the oldest written records are only 5,000 years old? Ages of caves dated before that time are not based upon written records. They are derived using assumptions which are at best unreliable, and deduced within an evolutionary framework. If early man had reproduced at virtually zero rate of population increase over the past one million years to today's population, then some three million, million people would have lived and died with almost no fossil remains or record of culture.

The world's oldest buildings demonstrate a considerable knowledge of architecture and astronomy. Egypt's Great Pyramid illustrates precise knowledge of geometry and astronomy possessed by man at the dawn of recorded history. Many of these early buildings are comprised of giant blocks of stone so well fitted that it is not possible to drive a knife blade between them. The calendar of the ancients was calculated with a precision only matched in the twentieth century AD.

Stone Age Cultures

Following the dispersion from the Tower of Babel, migrating tribes would, perforce, have adopted a simple life-style. Hunting and fruit gathering would have preceded agriculture and industry. The 'stone age' would have been a temporary stage before the peoples settled and built furnaces to smelt metal ores which they had mined. And these Stone Age men had evinced an advanced knowledge of astronomy as demonstrated at Stonehenge and in the stone circles of the British Isles and Brittany.

Present day stone age cultures have degenerated from a former more sophisticated civilization. An example of this degeneration is the South American Indian, a descendant of the former Mayan civilization.

Were the cave men of Chou Kou Tien, who ate the brains of Sinanthropus (the so-called Pekin Man) migrating from Babel? Evidence of Chinese civilization dates back to this time, with an astronomical reference in their *Book of History* assigned to 2,250 BC, the oldest recorded historical date outside of the Bible.

Ancient Tribal Histories

Many peoples claim to trace their ancestry back to Noah. The Arabs and Israelis trace their ancestries back to Noah through Shem. The Kurds also trace their people back to Noah. The king lists of the Irish Celts, the Saxons and the early Britons go back to Noah through Japheth. The Miao people of southwest China have a Creation poem, learned by heart and passed down orally from generation to generation. It is remarkably similar to the Genesis account and includes the names of several patriarchs from Adam to Japheth. But these world-wide records are generally regarded as mythical by conventional scholars.

Language

When we compare written with spoken English, we find that the language is changing with time. In one way it develops as new vocabulary is coined to meet new ideas, especially in science and technology. The syntax, on the other hand, becomes more streamlined. Chaucer and Shakespeare are difficult to read, not only because of changes in the words used, but due to the more complex sentence constructions of old English. Modern English is less precise than old English. The word 'you' is less precise than 'thee' and 'you' which differentiated singular and plural a few hundred years ago. Languages degenerate rather than becoming more complex. Today's English is much less precise than classical Greek and Latin from which it is, in part, derived. The idea that apes gradually developed speech, and that language became more sophisticated, is contrary to what we know of the change of language with time.

In spite of this, the experts experiment with monkeys, studying their social habits and chatter for signs of incipient humanity. One symposium reported; 'The more that is known about it, the less these systems seem to help in the understanding of human language.' In fact, the oldest known languages are complex and sophisticated, not at all like the popular notion 'Me Tarzan – you Jane.' Languages have devolved rather than evolved.

Men Distinct from Beasts

Man is physically like other animals in blood circulation, respiration, digestion and so on. His brain is also physically like that of the animals in its convolutions and electrochemical reactions. However, his thoughts and actions are governed by more than desires, fears and instincts. He can love selflessly and appreciate beauty. Animals are in a class apart from Shakespeare, Sibelius and Stalin!

All men have an instinct to worship God. All men recognize justice and fair play. They have a concept of 'good', yet do not measure up to even their own standards of what is right. On the contrary, there is a strong tendency in even the most saintly to choose evil. If man had descended from apes, good and bad would be less important than expediency. How, then, did man develop the 'fallen nature' which we all recognize? And if man has not 'fallen', then the crucifixion of Christ is meaningless. On the other hand, if man is a special creation in the image of God, and has fallen, we have an explanation of man's conflicting passions.

Man's history, relics of civilization, his languages, his very nature, all fit in with the Genesis record but clash with a proposed animal origin.

Stonehenge.

Chapter 14

All in a Day's Work

The world's oldest collection of books, the Bible, claims throughout its pages to be the written word of God – inspired by God. In those areas where its contents can be checked against present day knowledge, such as in the realms of history, archaeology and various branches of science, it cannot be faulted. However, or so it would seem from our education system and from the mass media, not so in the matter of origins.

Moses' Source Material

The book of origins, or 'Genesis', was written by Moses during the second millenium BC. It has to be asked where Moses obtained his detailed records, and a clue to that is found in the structure of this first book of the Bible. Genesis is composed of many sections, each section being rounded off by the phrase *'These are the generations of…'*

Chapter 2 verse 4 completes the story of the creation of the heavens and the earth by summing up; *'These are the generations of the heavens and the earth when they were created, in the day that the Lord God made the earth and the heavens.'*

The next section introduces Adam and Eve by name, recounts the Fall, the story of Cain and Abel, and the progeny of Cain during Adam's long life. The section is summed up in chapter 5 verse 1; *'This is the book of the generations of Adam.'* Evidently the first man wrote his family history in a book, which was preserved by Noah to be passed on ultimately to Moses.

The next section gives the family tree of the line through Seth to Noah. The world population became great. Violence increased and every imagination of the thoughts of men's hearts was only evil continually. God determined to judge the earth with a world-wide flood, (and Christ likens that situation to His own second coming in world-wide judgement). This section of Genesis is rounded off in chapter 6 verse 9 with the statement; *'These are the generations of Noah:'*

The same refrain is found for the sons of Noah, for Shem, Terah, Abraham, Ishmael and Isaac, Esau and Jacob. Then the second book of Moses, Exodus, commences *'Now these are the names of the children of Israel (or Jacob) which came into Egypt;'* It may be noted in passing that Matthew begins his account *'The book of the generations of Jesus Christ, the son of David, the son of Abraham.'*

Genesis, then, is not some vague folk-memory written down by Moses the politician as he moulded the ten tribes into one nation. It is seen in the light of the above to have the immediacy and authenticity of contemporary family records.

How Long is a Day?

The structure of the first chapter of Genesis is the account of six days of creation followed by a day of rest. Theistic evolutionists have attempted to expand these days to represent long ages. One difficulty with such an interpretation is that the fruit trees created on the third 'day' would have had to wait to be pollinated by the insects created on the sixth 'day'. If each day was much longer than 24 hours, the fruit trees would not outlast their first generation. Of course, day

Interdependence of bees and blossom.

can be used of an indefinite period, as in 'Things were different in my day.' Day is used in Genesis 2 verse 4 to mean the whole period of creation. However, in all the instances in Scripture where the word day is qualified by a numeral (as 'the third day', 'six days'), it always refers to a 24 hour period. In verse 5, day is defined as the hours of daylight in the very verse where the first day is mentioned. Moreover, the day is amplified as *'the evening and the morning'*. Then in Exodus 20, we are told that the Lord created all things in six days and rested on the seventh day. Interestingly, this is given as the reason why we also should work for six days and observe a sabbath rest. The same reason is repeated for good measure in Exodus 31, *'written with the finger of God'*. One would be hard placed to imagine how the Author of the Bible could explain more clearly than He has that all things were made in the space of six literal days.

Before the Beginning

Some may enquire what there was before the creation of space, time, matter and energy. If God created time, He is outside of time. He is referred to as the Eternal God. Being outside of time, He had no beginning, which answers the old question as to who made God. Since He created time, He does not need to use time in creating anything, but can bring things into existence instantaneously.

Jesus, in John 17, says that his Father loved Him before the foundation of the world. Perhaps only a plurality of Godhead can be called a God of love before any created beings were around to be loved. The Bible reveals that Christ, the Lamb of God, was *'slain before the foundation of the world'* and our names were written in the Book of Life before the foundation of the world. In other words, before creating man on the earth, God foresaw he would sin, and foresaw the penalty which would have to be paid to restore us to fellowship with Himself. Even so, He reckoned it worthwhile to create man. *'For the joy that was set before Him, Christ endured the cross, despising the shame.'*

Ancient but not Out-dated

On the first day, God creates time (the beginning), space (the heavens), matter (the earth), and energy (light). Man operates within a space-time-matter-energy continuum. Matter, occupying space, vibrates in time, and is inter-convertible with energy. Matter could not exist in isolation from space, time and energy.

The book of Job, written some 4,000 years ago, tells us that the earth hangs in space. *'He stretches out the north over the empty place, and hangs the earth upon nothing.'* Isaiah, written two and a half millenia ago, refers to the fact that the earth is like a ball. *'It is He who sits above the circle of the earth ... '*

The newly created earth appears to have been shrouded completely in water, devoid of structure and empty. The remainder of the first section of Genesis describes the structuring and filling of the earth.

Mind the Gap

Some have sought to insert the vast imagined ages of evolution between verses 1 and 2 of this chapter. This time gap would be many, many times greater than the whole of the rest of historical time, as recorded in the Bible. The last chapter of the Bible warns against adding to Scripture. The Lord Jesus, who created all things, refers to Adam and Eve as being created *'in the beginning'* (Matthew 19:4). This could hardly be said if such a time gap existed. Adam's son Abel is mentioned with reference to historical time *'since the foundation of the world'* (Luke 11:50).

A further difficulty with this 'gap theory' is that there would have been death before Adam sinned. Romans 5 says that *'by one man sin entered the world, and death by sin; and*

He hangs the earth upon nothing. (Job 26:7)

so *death passed upon all men, for that all have sinned:'*
1 Corinthians 15 tells us that *'by man came death'* and *'as in Adam all die, even so in Christ shall all be made alive.'* If there was death before Adam, there is no link between sin and death, implying that the death of Christ was not for our sins. This death of Adam was physical death as well as spiritual death, for God said *'dust thou art, and unto dust shalt thou return.'* Nor is this death confined to human death, allowing for the death of countless animals before man, for Romans 8 tells us that the whole creation was affected by the sin of Adam. It follows that the gap theory would completely undermine the gospel by breaking the link between death and sin. This argument applies also to the interpretation of days as long periods of time. Any compromise between evolution and creation flounders on this issue.

The Triune Godhead

Upon that dark, formless, empty, freshly created earth, the Spirit of God moved. John tells us that all things were made by Christ. The triune God, Father, Son and Spirit, works to create. The Trinity also works in re-creation. Only in one great work did the Godhead not act together. The opening verses to the epistle to the Hebrews speak of Christ as Creator, but go on to say that He *'by Himself purged our sins.'* Peter, perhaps remembering that chilling cry of God-forsakenness from the cross, says that Christ *'His own self bare our sins in His own body on the tree.'*

The Light of the World

That there was light before the creation of the sun, moon and stars on day 4, need not concern us. God is light. He is the Creator of light as well as the Creator of the sources of light. That there was evening and morning the first day means that the earth was set spinning on its axis. It is the rate of rotation of the earth that determines the length of the day, not the apparent movement of the sun round the earth.

It is implicit in this account that the earth was created spinning on its axis with light coming from a fixed direction. Those ancient civilizations who thought the earth was flat were unaware that while one half of the earth was illuminated, the other half would be in darkness. The true picture of the earth is also apparent in Luke 17. Here, the Lord Jesus Christ foretells His coming again to the earth in the last days. He speaks of that moment as a time when two people will be sleeping in a bed, and again as when two people will be working in the field. Yet we are told that He will come in a moment, in the twinkling of an eye. In other words, in one instant it can be night in one part of the world while being day on the other side of the globe. The biblical view of this aspect of astronomy is seen to be the correct one.

A spinning earth would have a magnetic field in readiness to deflect solar wind from the earth, and in anticipation of the navigational requirements of migrating creatures. The earth's magnetic field has been measured frequently since Gauss' first studies in 1835. It is found to be getting less and less intense, in an exponential decay. Only ten thousand years ago it would have been as strong as that of a magnetic star! Clearly the earth cannot be as much as ten thousand years old.

Chapter 15
Waters Above the Firmament

On the second and third days of creation, the formless, empty earth was structured in readiness to receive the plants and animals which would be created during this first week of time.

'*Let there be a firmament in the midst of the waters, and let it divide the waters from the waters.*' What is this firmament? Well, on the fifth day God made winged fowl to fly above the earth in the open firmament of heaven. Clearly this expanse refers to the atmosphere. However the waters above the atmosphere cannot refer to the clouds, since clouds are floating at various levels within the atmosphere.

The Thermosphere

We now know that above our stratosphere there exists a deep expanse of space, virtually empty, but at a temperature well in excess of the boiling point of steam. It has been remarked upon that this layer could have held a vast quantity of invisible, super-heated steam. Could this be the explanation of the waters above the firmament? If so, where are those waters today?

Greenhouse Effect

A water vapour canopy would affect the terrestrial environment in many ways. While water vapour is transparent to much of the sun's radiation, the water molecules absorb in the infra red region of the spectrum. This is because the bonds between atoms in the water molecules vibrate at this frequency band. Today the earth is warmed by sunlight, and radiates most of the energy back into space as heat, the lower frequency infra red radiation. If the early earth were initially swathed in a vast cocoon of water vapour, the earth would not have been able to radiate its heat back to the same extent as today. It would have been as though the earth were in a giant greenhouse, made, not of glass but steam.

Greenhouses produce lush vegetation with large healthy plants. The fossil remains of plants indicate that vegetation was indeed luxuriant in the past. The earth's atmosphere would have been almost uniformly warm, even at the poles, and again coal deposits in the far North and in Antarctica indicate that this was the case. There would have been no polar ice caps. There would have been no wind systems – a paradise free from storms. But this would also mean that there would have been no rain for the crops. In support of this scenario we read in the second chapter of Genesis that *'the Lord God had not caused it to rain upon the earth ... but there went up a mist from the earth, and watered the whole face of the ground.'* We also read of rivers, indicating a high water table with springs of water issuing from the ground.

A water vapour canopy would have protected the earth from harmful high-energy solar radiation. Such a deep layer of water vapour would also have added considerably to the atmospheric pressure. The use of nuclear submarines today has meant that men have been subjected to prolonged high pressure. It is found that cuts do not bleed profusely, but heal quickly under such conditions. It is also found that there is a slowing down of the heart rate as blood is able to deliver its oxygen to the muscles at higher partial pressure. Were these factors responsible for the great longevity of the early people? Before the time of the Flood in the days of Noah, men lived for over 900 years. Following the Flood life-spans dropped exponentially with time to our present level.

Cataclysmic Flood

It would seem then, if this conjecture is correct, that the greenhouse effect lasted up to the time of Noah. Then the waters above the firmament were somehow precipitated as torrential rain during 40 days. Ordinary clouds would not have been able to support such a prolonged world-wide downpour. When the contour lines of the present land masses are examined at a level of half the average depth of the present oceans, it is found that there is an excellent fit. It is as though before the original land mass divided up, there had been only half the present amount of sea. It would seem that when the waters were divided in Genesis 1, they were halved, with half of the present ocean water becoming a vast water vapour canopy. Imagine such a vast quantity of water bucketing down during 40 days! Small wonder that in the judgement of the Flood we read that the windows of heaven were opened! The severity of the Flood, rapidly burying living things, scouring the land surfaces and depositing huge layers of sediments, beggars description. It is a more credible explanation of the geological column with its fossils than the idea of a tranquil evolution over millions of years!

After the Flood, the earth would have been covered with soft saturated sediments. As the balance of land and ocean masses adjusted themselves to the redistribution of the weight of water, the land mass would have risen. The water, draining from the higher levels, would have gouged out massive valleys, much larger than the rivers which run through them under today's conditions. Similar systems have been observed on a small scale, following the eruption of Mount St. Helens in Washington State in 1980.

The Ice Age

Without the waters above the firmament, the earth would have cooled as it radiated heat back into space. The polar regions, receiving less heat from the sun, would have become very cold. The water-laden atmosphere over the sodden land would develop constant cloud systems which would have deposited masses of snow and ice at the poles. Ice, flowing under its own weight, would have spread out from the poles, enveloping the land in ice sheets. There is, of course, ample evidence from geology and archaeology of such an ice age in early human history. The book of Job, written soon after the Flood, has many references to snow and ice, though today the area where Job lived is not noted for snow and ice! The world's climate is still adjusting itself today. Over recent centuries there has been a progressive drying out of lakes and inland seas, and a spreading of desert zones. For instance, Marco Polo (ca. 1300 AD) came across large inland seas on his journey to China, which have since dried up, while in this century Lake Chad has all but disappeared.

One Super-continent

A further structuring of the earth occurred on the third day of creation, when God gathered the waters under the firmament together into one place and the dry land appeared. The inference is that the dry land was one super-continent. This accords with the reference to Peleg in whose days the earth was divided (Genesis 10:25). It also ties in with the shape of the continents today, as we have just seen. It seems unlikely that Moses had access to world maps, so this information was either an inspired guess against the odds, or historical information passed on in written records.

Circumscribed Diversity

With the separation of a land mass from the water, God created grass, herbs and fruit trees during the third day. Note that it was an instantaneous creation. God spoke vegetation into existence. Evolution theory would have sea creatures developing before plants, but that assumption is derived from the order of burial and fossilization by the world-wide flood. Note also that these first biological forms had their seed within themselves, so that each reproduced after its kind. This specifically rules out evolution of one kind into another. The diversity present within the genetic information of a grass provides for the development of many varieties to suit different conditions and to meet different needs. However, that same genetic information sets limits to the diversity, so that one cannot go on selecting endlessly. Each variety is restricted by the genetic information present in the basic kind. Time cannot produce new genetic codes not already present, nor can chance mutations provide new information. Chance mutations and time can only lead to a loss of information.

A Perfect Creation

At the end of the third day, God saw that it was good. The lilies of the field surpass in splendour even Solomon in all his glory! People sometimes say, 'How can I believe in God when there is so much that is wrong with the world?' Genesis 1 tells us repeatedly that God saw that the things He had made were good. It is man's sin that affected all aspects of this world; indeed the whole creation groans and travails waiting to be delivered from this bondage of corruption.

God saw that it was good.

Chapter 16

He Bringeth out Their Host by Number

Go out on a clear night, get away from the lights of town, and you will see about a thousand stars. A telescope will reveal the Milky Way as composed of myriads of stars. Under greater magnification, some objects are seen to be galaxies beyond our Milky Way. Radio telescopes and X-ray detectors reveal still more of the vastness of the sky, with clusters of galaxies. In 1989, great walls of galaxies, the largest objects ever observed, were discovered at the far limits of detection. The earth seems insignificant by comparison. The Psalmist said, '*When I consider the heavens ... what is man?*'

Some 2,000 years ago, God said to Abraham, '*I will bless you, and I will multiply your descendants as the stars of heaven and as the sand which is on the seashore.*' Only in modern times has it been realized that the number of stars in the sky is comparable with the number of grains of sand on the seashore – a vast unknowable number.

Relative Simplicity of Stars

It seems out of proportion that the creation of the earth is given centre-stage in Genesis, while these vast constellations are dismissed with the throw-away phrase '*He made the stars also.'* Creation involves an input of energy and information. Jeremiah 10:12 reminds us that *'He hath made the earth by His power, He hath established the world by His wisdom, and hath stretched out the heavens by His discretion.'* The earth with its complex structures and host of living forms required an input of a great deal of information for its creation. Stars, for all their size and numbers, are, by comparison, extremely simple. In the stars, hydrogen nuclei are combined to form helium, and the nuclei of other simple atoms may also be made by the fusion process. (Even man is able to use this process in the H bomb.) So from the perspective of creation, the stars are simpler than the earth and relatively less significant.

Signs and Seasons

The stars were given, on that fourth day of creation, for signs and seasons. The star groupings are easily recognizable, and the names of constellations and of individual stars have not changed from antiquity. It is said that the details of God's dealings with men are written in the stars. Virgo, Pisces and so on are part of the Gospel story. However, these signs have been corrupted by the occult, and God's Word commands us to avoid such things. How perverse of fallen man that he looks for daily guidance from the stars while the Word admonishes *'In all your ways acknowledge God, and He shall direct your paths.'*

Not only were the sun, moon and stars created for signs, but also for seasons. The ancient Egyptians measured the sidereal year using the brightest star Sirius. When the rising of this star occurred just at dawn, it also coincided with the annual flooding of the Nile delta at the height of summer. The array of stars appear to move around the heavens during the year but return to their same places after 365 days, 6 hours, 9 minutes and 9.6 seconds. Today we measure time by the frequency of atomic vibrations in the caesium clock, yet it has been shown that this atomic time is slowing down relative to time as measured by the movement of the heavenly bodies. The stars and the moon were used by the ancients for measuring the seasons which governed their agriculture. The relative positions of earth, moon and sun gave the phases of the moon which show the passage of days through the month. What a convenient clock-cum-calender, permanent and visible from any place on the globe. The apparent coincidence of sizes of the sun and moon as seen from the earth are dependent on their relative actual sizes and upon their distances from the earth. These factors, in turn, determine such effects as the earth's temperature and the height of tides. No wonder scientists say that the universe has the appearance of having been made for man.

Brightness of Thy Rising

David tells us in the 19th Psalm that the heavens declare the glory of God. The sun is likened to a bridegroom and to a strong man. Both allude to the coming Christ. He is stronger than, and able to bind, the strong man, and divide his spoils. For Him will come the midnight cry, 'Behold the bridegroom cometh, go ye out to meet him.' The closing chapter of the Old Testament also looks forward to the rising of the Sun of righteousness, with healing in his wings. The earth is entirely dependent on the sun for its life, since all its energy comes from the sun. In an analogous way, we are dependent on Christ, who is our life.

Fish and Fowl

On the fifth day, the first animal life was created. The word 'bara' (Hebrew – create) was used for the bringing into being of the initial time-space-matter. Following that, things were made or brought forth. Here a further novelty is created – conscious living things with personality, so bara is again used. We shall see that bara is used once more in the creation week when man is created in the image of God.

What a diversity was created on that day! The great sea creatures included the blue whale, largest living creature ever to inhabit the earth, as well as plesiosaurs such as the one fished up by the Japanese trawler off the coast of New Zealand on the 10th April, 1977. Some creatures of the sea use echo sounding devices while others can generate high voltages of electricity. Some, such as the octopus, can rapidly change colour to suit their surroundings, while some fish have beautiful colours even though they spend their time in the inky depths. Lord, how manifold are Thy works; in wisdom hast Thou made them all!

The winged fowl are also of mind-boggling diversity. The tiny bee humming bird weighs only two grams and beats its wings hundreds of times a second in flight. At night it lowers its body temperature to preserve energy. The arctic tern migrates halfway round the world from pole to pole, then flies back again. There are birds which achieve speeds of 150 mph in a dive, yet use updraughts of air to hover stationary while they survey the landscape with telephoto vision.

As with the vegetation on the third day, so with fish and fowl on the fifth day, they were all created after their kind. Evolutionists would have us believe that fish were the forerunners of land animals from which birds developed. They also imagine that some land mammals went back into the sea, exchanging limbs for fins again, to become whales and dolphins! Which scenario is more believable?

Kinds of Animals

On the sixth day the land creatures were formed; cattle, beasts and creeping things. More diversity. And between these created kinds, a network of interactions was set up, as pilot fish swam ahead of whales, and small fish cleaned the teeth of large fish. Insects and birds pollinated flowering shrubs and fruit trees. Evolutionists have a problem with symbiosis, as both partners in a relationship must evolve simultaneously and in a complementary fashion. In fact the

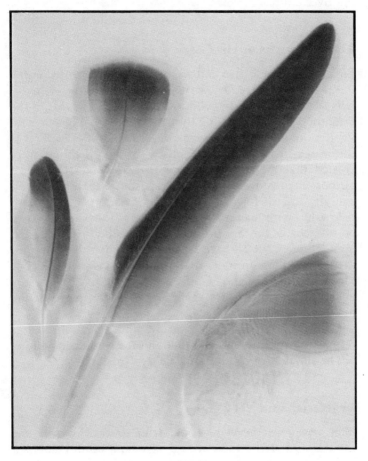

Feathers – designed for flight.

whole of nature is in balance, with the parts inter-dependent upon each other and upon the whole. This is why it was necessary for the whole of nature to be created together, and not over billions of years.

The Brightness of His Glory

Finally God made man and woman. Man was created in the image of the Creator. The writer of the letter to the Hebrews tells us that the Son, by whom God made the worlds, is the brightness of His glory and the express image of His person. Paul, writing to the Colossians, speaks of God's dear Son as the image of the invisible God by whom all things were created that are in heaven and that are in earth. God's purpose in creating all this, the stars, the earth, the sea, land and air, and all forms of life and vegetation, was to have fellowship with man made in His image. That image was to be marred by sin. Sin brought death, and so death passed upon all men, for all have sinned. Christ died for our sins, the just for the unjust, so that ultimately we might be conformed to the image of God's Son. As we have borne the image of the earthy, we shall also bear the image of the heavenly.

Man was given dominion over the whole creation. Man is responsible for this planet. It is not his to exploit and pollute, but he should exercise responsible stewardship over it.

Vegetarian and Very Good

Man was given vegetables and fruit to eat, as were the animals. Otherwise there would have been death before sin had entered the world. In the restored economy of God, we are told that the lion will eat straw like the ox, and they shall not hurt nor destroy, for the earth shall be full of the knowledge of the Lord, as the waters cover the sea.

And that is how it was in the beginning.

The Lion and the Lamb will lie down together. (Isaiah 11:6)

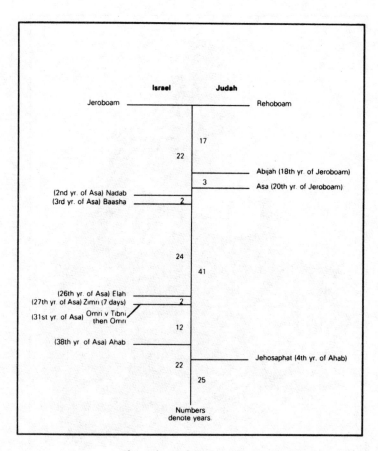

Chronology of Hebrew kings.

Chapter 17

History of Early Man

The book of Genesis gives a history of man from the Creation through to times which are also known from secular history. The time scale involved can be calculated using the genealogies of chapters 5 and 11 to give a date for the Creation of just about 4,000 BC.

Meticulous Chronologies

Some have said that these genealogies are not necessarily complete, so that the earth may be very much older than this. The dating of events in Scripture is carefully recorded, in contrast to those of other ancient peoples. Manetho's lists of Egyptian kings was written as late as 250 BC, and is only preserved in a few inaccurate quotations in other writings. However, in Scripture we have such statements as: *'The time that the people of Israel lived in Egypt was 430 years'; 'In the 480th year after the people of Israel came out of Egypt, in the fourth year of Solomon's reign over Israel, in the month of Ziv, which is the second month, he began to build the house of the Lord'; 'In the first year of Cyrus, king of Persia...'; 'In the fifteenth year of the reign of Tiberius Caesar...'*

Some genealogies in the Bible are simply lists of names in historical sequence which are clearly incomplete. For example, if we compare Ezra's family tree back to Aaron in Ezra 7 with the analogous list in 1 Chronicles 6, we find an extra six names in the latter. Since the writers are concerned to show descent and inheritance, completeness is not essential to their task. The longer list of the Chronicler fits the time span better. With other genealogies, extra details are given which indicate that the lists are complete, and that they can be used to measure the passage of time. The lists of the kings of Israel and Judah which are interspersed in the narrative matter of Kings and Chronicles are of this sort. For example; *'In the eighteenth year of Jehoshaphat king of Judah, Jehoram the son of Ahab became king over Israel in Samaria, and he reigned for twelve years.'*

Genealogies Complete

The genealogies of Genesis 5 and 11 have extra details, such as the age of the parent when the heir (not always the oldest son) was born. For example, we read that when Adam was 130 years old, he fathered Seth, that Adam lived a further 800 years after the birth of Seth, and that he lived a total of 930 years and then died. There is no room for ambiguity here, and we can build up a chart which enables us to add the years together, just as Ussher and others have done, to arrive at a date for the Creation of about 4,000 BC. Genesis 4 gives the line of Cain up to the time of Adam's death. (Genesis 5:1 indicates that the second, third and fourth chapters were written by Adam.) Jude refers to Enoch as the seventh from Adam, showing that this Early Church Father and half-brother of our Lord regarded the Genesis list as complete.

Variations in the Septuagint

In Luke 3:36, however, we find the name Cainan, which does not occur in 1 Chronicles 1. Luke, a Gentile physician, has taken as his source the Septuagint Version of the Torah. The Septuagint version in both Genesis 10:24 and 11:12 includes Cainan, adding a further 130 years to the tally. The

Septuagint has also added many years to the ages in the pre- and post-flood genealogies, so that Methuselah is made to survive the flood – a blatant inaccuracy. The Septuagint, the Greek translation of the Hebrew Old Testament, was published in Egypt shortly after Manetho's Egyptian chronology and it would seem that these scribes were pressurized to bring their time scale into line with that of Manetho. When one plots the ages of the post-flood patriarchs against time, one finds an approximately exponential decay of their life spans. The inclusion of Cainan throws the curve off the expected line. Further, the longer spans for post-flood lives as given in the Septuagint version give a linear decay to the life spans, contrary to expectation.

Almost Millenarians

The great ages of those who lived before the flood present a problem to modern man. Over the last 200 years, the life-expectancy of Western man has almost doubled, but today there still seems to be an upper limit of about 120 years beyond which no-one survives. The aging process is not understood, although breeding from fruit flies which are themselves old (rather than from young parents), has produced a longer-lived strain of flies which show genetic differences. Greater atmospheric pressure before the flood, and the presence of a radiation shield in the form of waters above the atmosphere, have been suggested as reasons for the longevity of antediluvian man. But we do not know for sure, because ever since Adam disobeyed, the way to the Tree of Life has been barred.

Some have suggested that the time periods in the Genesis genealogies were months rather than years, so that the mean of about 950 'years' becomes about 75 years. However, by such accounting, Enoch was only 65/13 or 5 years old when he fathered Methuselah, which is somewhat precocious!

Following the flood, there was a decay in the life spans as recorded in Genesis 11. Shem lived for six hundred years

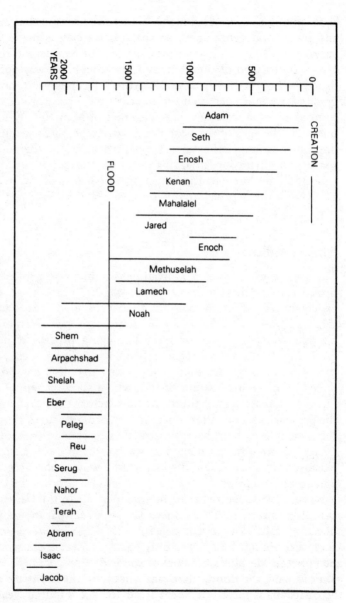

Ages of the Patriarchs.

while Abraham, born some three hundred and ninety years later, lived for one hundred and seventy-five years. Many of the post-flood patriarchs outlived their descendants. For instance, Shem outlived Abraham by about forty-five years, so that Jacob could say to the Pharaoh *'I'm 130 years old. Few have been my years, unlike my fathers.'*

First-hand Account

The folklore of many ancient people speak of long lived ancestors and a flood. It is claimed that the early chapters of Genesis are also folklore, passed down from one generation to the next, becoming embellished with the telling. However we can calculate from the genealogies that Methuselah could, and almost certainly would, have known every member of this family tree from Adam to Shem over hundreds of years of active life. This gives to the whole record the validity of a first-hand account. Again, after the flood, Noah and Shem were contemporary with Terah and Abraham. The writer to the Hebrews tells us that by faith, Abraham, when he was called to go out into a place which he would later receive as an inheritance, obeyed; and went out not knowing where he was going. How much more probable that this was not just blind faith, but faith based upon experience of a faithful God and the testimony of men like Noah and Shem.

Archaeological Confirmation

The great-grandson of Shem was Eber, born only sixty-seven years after the flood. He outlived six succeeding generations. He is known to archaeologists from inscriptions showing him to have been a leader of the people. Genesis 10:21 refers to Shem as the father of all the children of Eber, and from Eber's name the word 'Hebrews' is derived. Eber called his son Peleg, which means 'divided', for in his days the earth was divided (Genesis 10:25).

'One Day as a Thousand Years'

Archaeology, history, folklore and statistics all suggest that the genealogies are an accurate and complete account of the early history of mankind. This gives a date for the creation of about 4,000 BC. Prophecies concerning the second coming of the Lord Jesus Christ strongly suggest that we, at the close of the sixth millenium, live in the last days. Perhaps it is not fanciful to relate the six days of Creation to the six thousand years of history, and the sabbath rest to the coming millenial reign. When He comes, will the Creator find the education system and the media still preaching evolution theory? Will He find His church still compromising over this basic issue? Must we wait until that old serpent is bound for a thousand years before his first lie, 'Hath God said?', is finally repudiated?

Index

What is CSM all about?

The Creation Science Movement started in 1932 protesting about the influence of Darwin's theory of evolution; in fact it was called the Evolution Protest Movement in those days.

The prime movers were Mr Douglas Dewar, barrister and Auditor General of the Indian Civil Service, and Captain Bernard Acworth, DSO who developed the asdic sonar device (Who's Who). They called the first Creationist meeting (EPM) at 21 Essex Gardens, The Strand, London, in 1932. The first public meeting was reported in *The Times* on February 12, 1935. Sir Ambrose Fleming presided and what he said then still stands for what the Creation Science Movement believes in today. He declared that 'of late years the Darwinian anthropology had been forced on public attention by numerous books ... in such a fashion as to create a belief that it was a certainly settled scientific truth. The fact that many eminent naturalists did not agree that Darwin's theory of species production had been sufficiently established as a truth was generally repressed. If there had been no creation, there was no need to assume any Creator; the chief basis for all religion was taken away and morality reduced to mere human expediency. It had seemed to a large number of thoughtful persons that it was of national importance to ... counteract the effects of the reckless and indiscriminate popularisation of the theory of the wholly animal origin of mankind, especially among the young, by the diffusion of a truly scientific ... cause for all those altruistic, aesthetic, intellectual, spiritual and religious faculties ... in man, of which not the very slightest trace was seen in the animal species ... they desired to oppose a one-sided materialistic presentation of human origin which rejected altogether any suggestion of creation ... They said that the arguments of the Darwinian anthropologists were defective in logic and did not give the proof they assumed'.

This was reported over half a century ago! Today society witnesses to the effect of atheistic humanism which belief in the theory of evolution has brought – fragmented family units, abortion, child abuse etc.

In fact in all these intervening years the evidence has mounted up arguing that of course a Creator must have made this planet Earth and the heavens. There is a wealth of further scientific evidence supporting Creation which these eminent men in the early 1930s did not then know. Advances in our knowledge of genetics, biochemistry and information theory are just some areas where progress in the last sixty years has made belief in evolution even less logical.

The sense of high purpose expressed in *The Times* account is still what motivates CSM today. We are concerned that people today are rarely confronted with a straightforward reading of the Bible starting at Genesis chapter one. In fact most people have been told that they cannot trust the beginning of God's Word. They rehearse Satan's own words, 'Hath God said?'. CSM declares that the doctrine of original sin is not based on myth or fable but rather on the solid foundation of the 'lively oracles' of the Lord God. A blurring of this truth affects the wonder of the Atonement by the peerless Son of God which in turn can lead to a shallow commitment to Him. CSM ringingly declares that the beginning of God's Word may be trusted as well as all that follows.

What else does CSM do? A pamphlet on different subjects giving evidence of Creation is published every other month together with the *Creation Journal* which carries up-to-the-minute news and comment. These pamphlets form an information resource on the Creation/evolution issue. One of our pamphlets shows how Creation is the foundation of the Gospel (249) while others trace Creation in Genesis (260) and Isaiah (243). Others are critical of aspects of evolution theory such as alleged vestigial organs (258) and supposed intermediate forms such as Archeopteryx (76) and ape-men (151, 234). Many pamphlets consider particular creatures and show how they could not possibly have evolved. These include whales (114) where the design of the mouth of the young whale fitting into the mother enables it to be suckled while at sea. The Bombardier Beetle (233) had to have a perfectly functioning explosive defence or it would have blown itself up! The Palisade moth (248), birds' feathers (255), bats' sonar systems (247), the bees' informative dance (264), and butterflies' metamorphoses (257) could not have evolved. Other pamphlets consider the so-called chemical evolution of life (267). Evidence is cited that the universe is only thousands of years old (265). Measurements of salinity of the oceans (221) show they are young. The eruption of Mount St. Helens (252) in 1980 produced sediments which evolutionary geologists would normally interpret as taking very long periods of time to form. Three distinct lines of experimental evidence from scientists of repute in Australia, America and Russia strongly suggest that the speed at which light travels has diminished with time (262 & 256). This affects the radiometric dating of rocks (207) and the time taken for light to reach us from distant galaxies. It indicates that the universe is less than 10,000 years old. Scientific observations support the genealogies (219) in the Bible, a book of amazingly accurate science (254), that life was created and did not evolve and that Adam was created in the beginning.

CSM provides able speakers on Creation who major on the scientific evidence which is increasingly weighty. Today many eminent scientists who do not even argue from the Christian standpoint, find this evidence against the theory of evolution sufficient to convince them that there is no evolution at all. This evidence is ignored in school textbooks and TV nature programmes. CSM lecturers regularly address universities, colleges, sixth forms and Church groups throughout the UK. In the 1960s our Creationist speakers toured the Far East, Australia, New Zealand and North America, while in the 1990s we are beginning to meet the need in Eastern Europe.

The Creation Resources Trust at Yeovil, which maintains close links with CSM, is able to offer a wide selection of creationist books, slides, tapes and videos. CRT publish attractive creationist papers for children and teens, which are also distributed by ourselves.

CSM has Charitable status (Charity no: 801745). We are members of the Evangelical Alliance. May we admit that we need you as a member. The hard-nosed humanism of evolutionism has become entrenched in the British educational system and in society at large. We need your dedicated support to topple it! Your subscription will help: and if you could arrange a meeting as well, even better!

At heart CSM wishes to give glory to the Lord Jesus Christ who created man in the image of the Triune God and then stooped to redeem us.

☐ Please enrol me as a Member of CSM.
☐ I enclose £5 subscription ⎫
☐   £3 student   ⎬ [1991–1992 prices]
☐   £6 if overseas ⎭
☐ I enclose £1 for sample literature

(PLEASE PRINT)

Name ....

Address ....

....

.... Postcode ....

Distribution Address:
Creation Science Movement
50 Brecon Avenue
Cosham, Portsmouth
PO6 2AW
England